How I Achieved Real Success

How I Achieved Real Success

A HAPPINESS GUIDE FOR MODERN WOMEN

INDIRA MESHRAM

Bhakti Vikas Trust

ISBN 978-93-82109-60-0

beingwomentoday
www.beingwomentoday.com
beingwomentoday@gmail.com

The words *Conversation, Lecture, Letter,* and *purport* indicate quotations taken from published editions by or involving Śrīla Prabhupāda. *Conversation* subsumes all types of discussions with Śrīla Prabhupāda, variously classified by the Bhaktivedanta Archives as Morning Walks, Press Conferences, Room Conversations, etc. All such quotations are copyrighted by The Bhaktivedanta Book Trust International, Inc.

Published by:
Bhakti Vikas Trust,
Surat, India
books.bvks.com; books@bvks.com
+(91)-7016811202

Printed in India

To the women in my life
and in the pages of *Śrīmad-Bhāgavatam*
who inspired me to seek real success.

Contents

Preface

Summer, 2017. We decided to spend our annual vacation in America. One of the highlights of the trip was meeting my extended family. It was pleasant to catch up with first cousins whom I had met only sporadically since they had relocated from India more than two decades ago. As we watched the children happily playing together, we reminisced about our own childhood — endless summer vacations, when my family and those of my three aunts would descend on my grandmother's house in Delhi, and nine children aged between five and fifteen would create complete mayhem.

Our reunion was progressing as expected, with much gossiping about family members who were not present, and yet there was an underlying tension that completely escaped me until my cousin-sister launched into a long tirade. She began to question my life choices. Among all the cousins, I was considered to be the most intelligent, and yet why had I chosen not to work? Why did I have such a courteous attitude towards my husband — to the extent that I did not even address him by his first name? Why had we decided to live in a small community and educate our children in the local school? She even complained about me being too careful about my children's diet, based on the fact that I had requested her to bring fresh fruits (and not frozen or *imported* ones) when she was going to the supermarket.

What surprised me was not that she should question my choices (which is something I face often), but that she was so angry about them. She was absolutely livid! And yet, there was no indication that either my children or I were unhappy in any way, so I wondered what she was so upset about.

Perhaps she considered the fact that I was following a more traditional lifestyle was evidence enough that I must be horribly repressed by my husband, and being a close relative felt indignant on my behalf.

Or, perhaps, I was witnessing a defensive reaction — the frustrated fury of a working woman struggling to bring up three little girls.

Perhaps it was a bit of both. But her reaction made me realize how disconnected my generation is from the principles of traditional culture. She was so convinced that there could be no rational explanation for my way of life that she didn't even bother to hear my side of the story before delivering her verdict that it would have a long-term damaging effect on me and my children.

I don't blame her. I know where she's coming from. I was there, twenty years ago.

****

I grew up in an era of great social change in India. The social and economic reforms post-independence had resulted in better facilities for education, created more jobs in the cities, and had, inadvertently, resulted in the breakdown of the joint family system. My parents' generation was well-read and aware of societal changes the world over. Global travel was becoming more common, and people began to go abroad for employment.

My parents were fond of books and Western music — interests that I automatically inherited.

At that time, another phenomenon influenced people's thinking like nothing else had in the past — the television. Suddenly, images from all over the world were projected into everyone's houses, and the media — through news bulletins, entertainment programs and movies, and even advertisements — gained control of the common man's mind like no political or social movement had been able to do previously. One of the things that happened, as a result, was that the social changes in the Western countries began to be mirrored in the developing countries as well.

While the women's movement had already been active in India for several decades — beginning with social reformers in the British era, who encouraged educated women to form women's organizations — in the late 1970s, it became mainstream with the emergence of new women's groups in cities like Delhi, Bangalore, and Bombay. Although these organizations focused on local issues such as child marriage and widow remarriage in the beginning, under the influence of their international counterparts, they began propagating ideals of equal opportunity to work.

Thus, although our college-educated mothers themselves adhered to the traditional role of being homemakers, they envisioned a very different future for their daughters.

From the very beginning, I knew that I would go to work after finishing my education. Since I was good at Math and Science, I was encouraged to aspire to be an engineer just like my father. We were told to be bold and independent, and much praise was showered on girls who won prizes at school in debates or elocution. People would ask the children, "What

My mother always encouraged me and my elder sister to be independent and "capable of standing on our own two feet."

do you want to be when you grow up?" and both boys and girls were expected to come up with grand career options like 'doctor' or 'pilot,' and to spend the rest of their childhood working towards achieving that goal. Unlike their previous generation, parents were no longer scanning matrimonial advertisements when their children turned 18, but instead were researching the admission criteria of various colleges. After receiving their graduate (and sometimes postgraduate) degrees, their adult children would job-hop for the next few years to land a well-paying job, while the parents would look on approvingly. As a result, within a generation, the average age of getting married shot up from 16 to 24 years for girls, and from 20 to 28 for boys.

As it happened, I did end up in an engineering college, enrolled in one of the most coveted courses at the time — computer science. Staying on the campus far from home, traveling with friends on trains during vacations, managing my finances and studies, and in general being free to do whatever I wanted — which in large part included activities like going out to parties or rock concerts — I decided it was good to be an independent woman and pitied all the oppressed women in the past who had to remain home-bound. My friends and I devoured Ayn Rand's books, and spent many hours discussing her philosophy. We were pleased to be part of the generation who, like Roark,[1]

College life was an endless stream of parties and 'excursions.'

1. The protagonist in Ayn Rand's novel *The Fountainhead*.

would break conventions and wouldn't hesitate to express our individuality.

After I graduated and settled into my first job, and experienced the thrill of having my very own money to spend, I figured life could only get better.

It did — although not quite as I had expected.

One day, I met a young man, and as we became friends, he would often engage me in conversation on a topic I had not given much thought to: spirituality. I admitted I had faith in God, but as he probed further, I realized that my faith was purely sentimental and not based on any real philosophy. He gave me books which explained the scientific basis of religion. It appealed to my rational mind for I was not expected to 'just believe.' These books were written by A.C. Bhaktivedanta Swami Prabhupāda, a saint in the ancient Gauḍīya Vaiṣṇava tradition and the founder of ISKCON, the International Society for Krishna Consciousness. Śrīla[1] Prabhupāda had painstakingly translated the Vedic texts[2] into English, and written commentaries, so

---

1. Just as Mr. and Ms. are prefixed to names of men and women, the Sanskrit word 'Śrīla' is used to show respect and reverence to an eminent personality.

2. The *Vedas* are a vast body of knowledge that cover both material and spiritual aspects of human life. At the present time, Vedic culture is incorrectly equated with Indian culture. Although it is true that the Indian subcontinent has been the hub of Vedic culture since time immemorial, and currently followers of this culture are found predominantly in the Indian subcontinent, the version of culture we see today in India is far removed from the high ideals that epitomize Vedic culture. From the Vedic scriptures we learn that centuries ago this was the predominant culture throughout the world, but with time its influence has diminished.

that the valuable knowledge contained in them would be easily accessible to everyone. He explained that life was not meant simply for working hard to have a comfortable standard of living, but primarily to understand who we are, who God is, and what our relationship with Him is.

What struck me the most was that Śrīla Prabhupāda emphasized that spiritual self-realization was not a vague, 'pie in the sky' sort of a concept that men sitting in armchairs puffing on cigars should be debating about, but, in fact, it is real, can be experienced firsthand by anyone who is sincere, and should be an essential part of our everyday lives.

As I became more and more interested, I was inspired to practice *sādhana* – the regular devotional program – which would help to further enhance my new understanding. Śrīla Prabhupāda often used to say that the proof of the pudding is in the eating. Indeed, as I began to follow the Vedic instructions, my conviction grew, for I could see that my consciousness was changing, and overall, I was happier and more serene than I have ever been.

Yet it wasn't easy, for it seemed that the ideals of spiritual life were quite the opposite of the beliefs held dear by most people, including me. The *Vedas* exhort people to be humble, satisfied in all circumstances, noble in their thoughts, and kind to all living entities. These are, without doubt, praiseworthy qualities, but actually they are no longer appreciated in the present society. The message we received while growing up was to be fiercely competitive and always strive to achieve more – a better job, a fancier car, and a bigger house. The implicit message was that it would be nice if this could be achieved without hurting anyone in the bargain, but if things do get nasty along the way, so be it. As I began to understand the importance of qualities such as humility and compassion, I reconciled to the fact that a large part of my spiritual life would be spent in the attempt to undo the harmful attitudes which I had internalized earlier.

A related challenge, for me personally, was to understand and accept my role as a woman according to the Vedic tradition.

In the Vedic culture, spirituality is a way of life: it's not something that one engages in once a week on Sunday. Therefore, the Vedic scriptures not only provide a set of rituals for worshiping God, but they also circumscribe various facets of one's life right from early childhood to the time one has to leave one's body, for aspects of worship are intertwined even in day-to-day activities. The structure of the society; the duties of men and women; the responsibilities of the king, the priests, the farmers, the traders, the artisans — everything is dealt with in great detail, so that people's lives can be structured in such a way that the spiritual goal is not forgotten.

In his commentaries, Śrīla Prabhupāda often deals with these aspects, including the role of women in society. At first, I found it very difficult to accept his statements, for they seemed to be the complete opposite of the ideals that I had set for myself. However, I realized that they are not his personal opinions. His comments are based on ancient wisdom given in the Vedic scriptures. I could understand that the *Vedas* provide the blueprint for a harmonious life, and hence, the role defined for each individual would work for their benefit. So I decided to examine the subject of women in Vedic culture further, to try and figure out how the principles could be reconciled with my own life.

I focused on parts of the Vedic scriptures relating to women and tried to assimilate the message. I studied the position of women in Vedic society. I noticed that in India each generation was drifting further and further away from Vedic traditions, but the modern culture had failed to deliver the fulfillment it had promised. I noted that we had turned away from our traditions in disappointment, seeing them used as an excuse for exploitation. And yet, on studying the scriptures, I realized that the problem lies not in the practice, but in the practitioners; not in the culture, but in the misuse of it. Somewhere along the way the rituals had remained but the object of following them — to please the Supreme Lord — had been lost.

I noticed a peculiar dichotomy in India. Even though my parents and grandparents were following Vedic culture in some shape and form, they did not have a deep understanding of it, and consequently, neither did they feel it necessary to convey it to us coherently, nor stood in the way when the modern value system started, slowly but surely, replacing our traditions. Enamored by the contemporary worldview, they were liberal in our upbringing. But, at the same time, they were reluctant to completely abandon their culture, and sentimentally clung to the hope that we would continue the tradition. They wanted us to be pushy career women and submissive wives and daughters-in-law, all at the same time. For most of us, however, the balance was tilted away from the traditional model.

Still, I could appreciate that even though the older generation did not know in great detail the whys and wherefores of Vedic culture, they had strong faith in their culture and followed it almost intuitively. I observed the behavior of older ladies in my family (which was a large sample set in itself), who were consciously or unconsciously adhering to Vedic culture, and was impressed by their grace and simplicity, and the level of peacefulness in their life. I am indebted to them, for they showed me, by their practical example, the ideals of sacrifice, patience, and kindness that I had read about in the scriptures.

I began to look more closely at cultures which were not practicing the values as given in the *Vedas* and studied the consequences of their not doing so. I observed that a startling number of women were confused and stressed. I examined my own life and my level of satisfaction before and after I had started to follow traditional culture. On scratching the surface of the happiness of the independent woman that I was, I found loneliness and insecurity, and a kind of brittle hardness that was frightening. On the other hand, when I surrendered to following the instructions of the *Vedas* and accepting a more submissive role, I felt I was more in touch with what it means to be a woman.

After a few years of hearing Śrīla Prabhupāda's lectures and reading his books, I gained an appreciation of Vedic culture which completely changed my worldview. To quote P. G. Wodehouse, I felt that the scales had fallen from my eyes! All my life I had been completely dismissive of even the vestiges of Vedic culture that I could see around me, considering them to be primitive traditions that must be given up to make way for modernity. And yet, through Śrīla Prabhupāda's insight, I began to see that the culture was there to facilitate harmony between material and spiritual life. This understanding was further enhanced when I encountered the teachings of one of Śrīla Prabhupāda's disciples, Bhakti Vikāsa Swami, who painstakingly explains how principles of traditional culture can be practically applied in the current context and emphasizes that they are as relevant today as they were centuries ago.

My research and introspection helped me to accept the Vedic view. I have seen my life transform and feel so grateful for having a level of contentment I had not experienced previously. However, it has been a long and arduous journey, and it certainly would have been easier if I had known then what I know now. I was never one to accept things at face value and spent a long time questioning every aspect of Vedic culture related to women. Fortunately, I received an explanation for

Content and Happy

every apprehension that I had, and my skepticism was replaced with enthusiasm.

I spent the first twenty years of my life trying to fit in with the hip, modern culture and the next twenty years living according to Vedic culture, instead. This book is an attempt to share what I have read and experienced in order to offer some food for thought to other women like me, who are trying to make sense of the contradictions around us. It is meant for those who are following Vedic tradition and would like to know more about their heritage. This book is for those who are curious about ancient traditions. It is also for those who are disparaging of them, if they are open-minded enough to have some of their theories questioned.

Although I am specifically discussing Vedic culture, the principles can be similarly applied to other traditional cultures all over the world. Therefore, I hope women from diverse backgrounds will be able to relate to this presentation of traditional versus modern values. My intention is to remove misconceptions that currently surround traditional culture, by presenting the principles and explaining how they were implemented in bygone days to create an environment for everyone to thrive in their individual capacities.

This presentation may assist the readers to regard traditional culture with less suspicion and scorn; it may even help women modify their lives in such a way that they are happier and more peaceful, however, my main motivation for inspiring women to re-examine traditional culture is not just for them to be materially more comfortable, but for them to be in a situation which is most conducive for their spiritual life. I would like them to consider a way of life that gives them the breathing space to read the scriptures, the peace of mind to contemplate what they have read, the time to enhance their devotional practice, and the fulfillment of sharing their realizations with their family and friends.

At this stage, I would like to emphasize that because our presentation is focused on women, it should not be taken to mean that men are off the hook! Obviously, since we are functioning in a society, the roles of men and women are interconnected. The onus of bringing about a positive moral and cultural change sits squarely on the shoulders of both the genders. In the analysis which follows, the complementary role that men need to play to facilitate women in their duties will also be discussed. However, the topic of men's duties is a large one in itself and to delve deeply into it is beyond the scope of this book.

Throughout the book I present the Vedic view, giving references from Vedic scriptures, particularly the *Śrīmad-Bhāgavatam*.[1] Of all the Vedic literatures, the *Śrīmad-Bhāgavatam* is considered to be the most authoritative, because its eighteen thousand verses, written by the compiler of the *Vedas*, Vyāsadeva, serve as his commentary on the *Vedānta-sūtra*, the essence of all theistic knowledge. I also refer to Śrīla Prabhupāda's commentaries[2] and his remarks in conversations and letters,[3]

---

1. *Śrīmad-Bhāgavatam*, English translation and commentary by His Divine Grace A.C. Bhaktivedanta Swami Prabhupāda (Los Angeles: The Bhaktivedanta Book Trust, 1972).
2. Such references will be footnoted as 'purport by Śrīla Prabhupāda' preceded by the verse he has commented on.
3. To read the full transcript of the lectures, conversations and letters please visit www.vanipedia.org

since he is considered to be an authority on Vedic culture, not only due to his extensive study of the Vedic scriptures and strict adherence to the Vedic tenets throughout his life, but also due to his deep realizations on the subject matter. Subsequently, I examine the consequences of not following traditional culture in terms of its impact on the well-being of women. For this, I sample the Western countries since the last century has witnessed Western society's rejection of the traditional role for women. I also felt it was important to scrutinize this culture in particular, for at present the Western countries are the perceived leaders in setting trends for the rest of the world to follow. I present some views of contemporary thinkers in these countries in the course of my analysis.

Today, we women are indeed in a unique position of holding the power to make our own life choices. We are encouraged to think for ourselves and draw our own conclusions. I hope the ideas presented in this book will help us make better-informed decisions on how we wish to shape our lives and the lives of those around us.

Introduction

The past century has seen the Western countries, particularly America and Britain, rise to great prominence. Today, most countries look up to the Western world in awe and are eager to try and adopt its value system and lifestyle. It is no surprise then that the prevalent mood in the Western countries is rapidly reflected in other places. One of the most prominent issues has been that of women's role in society. The feminist movement has changed the face of the Western society dramatically since the late nineteenth century, and has gradually been sweeping through the rest of the world as well. However, many of the ideals of modern Western life are in sharp contrast with the culture and traditions that have been extant for centuries. In the eagerness to jump onto the bandwagon and embrace the 'civilized' Western way of thinking, countries in Asia and Africa risk completely turning their backs on their own rich heritage.

Every country and its people have something unique to offer. Śrīla Prabhupāda suggested that the East and West cooperate together in order to create a peaceful, God-centered world. Using the analogy of the blind man and the lame man, *andha-paṅgor nyāya*, he explained that the material opulence of the West should be complemented by the cultural wealth of the East:

> India could not improve on account of poverty, lame. And America? Blind for want of culture. So let the blind man carry the lame man on the head, and the lame man give direction that "Go this way," and he walks. So both men's work is done. There is no hampering because one is blind and one is lame. Combined together, they get the benefit. *Andha-paṅgor nyāya.*[1]

Traditionally, a little girl would remain close to her mother, playing with other girls in the neighborhood, and often spending a lot of time with younger siblings. After marriage, she would be under the wing of the older women in her husband's family, and would soon be busy in her role of being a wife, a mother and a daughter-in-law. As she matured, she would soon assume the responsibility of running the entire household, which in the case of joint families and an entourage of household help would be no less challenging than running a current-day start-up. When her children grew up and married, she would happily hand over her charge to the younger women in her family, and devote her time to spiritual pursuits. Such

---

1. Room Conversation, June 28, 1976.

a lady would be the source of wisdom and a calming influence on the family. Till the end of her life she would be surrounded by loving family members.

However, this is a far cry from the life of a woman today. The girls are taught that they must realize their potential by going beyond the confinement of their homes. The society, and particularly the media, has fostered the idea that to be 'just a housewife' is simply unacceptable. The women, being equal to men in every respect, must be allowed, encouraged, and in cases of resistance given special privileges by law, so that they are able to take their rightful place beside the men, in every sphere of life. Today, a girl spends the first twenty years of her life studying and the next forty years working. Somewhere in between, she may get married and have children, but if and when that happens depends upon how she is able to fit it into her grand plan of life. We are told that this, in fact, is the process of women's empowerment, and that after centuries of being sidelined, women are finally being heard and are getting their due. Clearly, the generations before us had it figured out all wrong, but fortunately, now everything is falling into place.

Except that it isn't.

Śrīla Prabhupāda noted:

> Actually, in the Western countries at least we see that the woman class, they want equal rights with men. And there is. There is no distinction. But it is my experience, the woman class, they are not happy in the Western countries.[1]

1. Lecture by Śrīla Prabhupāda, December 8, 1972.

Statistics substantiate Śrīla Prabhupāda's observation. A study conducted by economists Betsey Stevenson and Justin Wolfers entitled 'The Paradox of Declining Female Happiness' analyzes data regarding happiness trends in citizens of the United States and other industrialized countries from 1970 to 2005. It states "By many objective measures the lives of women in the United States have improved over the past 35 years, yet we show that measures of subjective well-being indicate that women's happiness has declined both absolutely and relative to men. The paradox of women's declining relative well-being is found across various datasets, measures of subjective well-being, and is pervasive across demographic groups and industrialized countries."[1]

Feminists would be quick to point out that it simply confirms their claim that the women are unhappy because of being discriminated against and still much needs to be implemented regarding achieving equality. But, as pointed out in the paper, objective measures clearly demonstrate that the women's movement has been successful in achieving many of their goals: "the gender wage gap has partly closed; educational attainment has risen and is now surpassing that of men; women have gained an unprecedented level of control over fertility; technological change in the form of new domestic appliances has freed women from domestic drudgery; and women's freedoms within both the family and market sphere have expanded." And so the paradox: "Given these shifts of rights and bargaining power from men to women over the past 35 years, holding all else equal, we might expect to see

1. Stevenson, Betsey, and Justin Wolfers. "The Paradox of Declining Female Happiness." *American Economic Journal: Economic Policy* 1, no. 2 (2009): 190–225.

a concurrent shift in happiness towards women and away from men. Yet we document in this paper that measures of women's subjective well-being have fallen both absolutely and relatively to that of men."

In the interest of women's happiness, therefore, it may prove beneficial to let our guard down and retrace our steps to try and figure out what went wrong. Are traditional values so harmful to a woman's general well-being that they must be completely eradicated? The past few decades have attempted to do just that and so far the results have not been encouraging.

This book intends to examine aspects of Vedic culture, particularly related to women, and discuss their relevance in today's world. It is an attempt to bring back into focus the glories of a culture that has God in its center and is based on ideals of a harmonious society where everyone is satisfied due to being situated in a position appropriate to their nature.

Respect and Protection

Women have a special place in Vedic culture. They are cherished and protected. It is believed that women, as the embodiment of Lakṣmīdevī, the goddess of fortune, are instrumental in bringing prosperity to the family.

Until recently, it was the case in cultures all over the world that women were responsible for keeping house and raising children. Generally, their contribution was considered invaluable in society and they were held in high regard for their selfless service attitude towards the family. Famous sayings such as 'the hand that rocks the cradle rules the world' both acknowledge and convey respect for women's priceless contribution in raising responsible children, which in turn helps build a stable society.

In *Śrīmad-Bhāgavatam*, Kaśyapa Muni praises his wife as follows:

> As one can cross over the ocean with seagoing vessels, one can cross the dangerous situation of the material ocean by living with a wife. O respectful one, a wife is so helpful that she is called the better half of a man's body because of her sharing in all auspicious activities. A man can move without anxiety entrusting all responsibilities to his wife. As a fort commander very easily conquers invading plunderers, by taking shelter of a wife one can conquer the senses, which are unconquerable in the other social orders. O queen of the home, we are not able to act like you, nor could we repay you for what you have done, even if we worked for our entire life or even after death. To repay you is not possible, even for those who are admirers of personal qualities.[1]

Śrīla Prabhupāda comments on how men and women complement each other.

> Actually, a woman is supposed to be the energy of the man. Historically, in the background of every great man there is either a mother or a wife. One's household life is very successful if he has both a good wife and mother. In such a case, everything about household affairs and all the paraphernalia in the house becomes very pleasing.[2]
>
> In other words, the wife is the inspiration of all good intelligence. [...] When a person is too anxious about family affairs, he cannot discharge his family duties nicely. A wife is therefore supposed to be an inspiration and should keep the husband's intelligence in good order so that they can

1. *Śrīmad-Bhāgavatam* 3.14.18–21.
2. *Śrīmad-Bhāgavatam* 4.26.15, purport by Śrīla Prabhupāda.

> combinedly prosecute the affairs of family life without impediment.[1]

One of the important duties of women was to abide by scriptures, follow the religious tenets and teach the word of God to the children. Such pious ladies have been glorified throughout scriptures. Women were honored as upholders of moral standards and spiritual practices.

Undeniably, women in traditional cultures were restricted (in order to offer them proper protection), and were expected to be reserved and submissive. Nevertheless, in Vedic culture, dignified womanhood has always been revered as a manifestation of the divine feminine nature. Pristine Vedic society recognized that genuine civilization can exist only where chaste, dutiful women are protected, respected, and cared for well. Women are to be especially honored for their irreplaceable contribution as mothers.

In Vedic culture one of the most oft-quoted sayings about women is *mātṛ-devo bhava*: "Be one for whom the mother is a god."[2] Every woman except one's own wife should be treated as one's mother. As Śrīla Prabhupāda often quoted (from Cāṇakya Paṇḍita), *mātṛvat para-dāreṣu:* "One should consider another's wife to be one's mother."[3]

Another famous maxim is:

> *yatra nāryas tu pūjyante ramante tatra devatāḥ*
> *yatraitās tu na pūjyante sarvās tatrāphalāḥ kriyāḥ*

1. *Śrīmad-Bhāgavatam* 4.27.2, purport by Śrīla Prabhupāda.
2. *Taittirīya Upaniṣad* 1.1.20.
3. See e.g. *Śrīmad-Bhāgavatam* 8.9.4, purport by Śrīla Prabhupāda.

> "Where women are honored, the gods rejoice, and where women are not revered, all undertakings become fruitless."[1]

In the *Mahābhārata,* on his deathbed Grandfather Bhīṣma warned Yudhiṣṭhira that if daughters or daughters-in-law were saddened due to ill-treatment, the entire dynasty would be destroyed. The *Mahābhārata,* in fact, recounts the historical events which led to the destruction of the Kauravas due to their insulting Draupadī and attempting to disrobe her.

The popular notion these days is that women throughout the ages have been taken for granted and treated as doormats. But as recently as a couple of generations ago, the family unit was considered the most important building block of a successful nation, and the role of a woman as a mother and a wife was genuinely appreciated. Even though they preferred not to come into the limelight, their contribution was considered invaluable: "Behind every successful man is a woman."

Protection: Treasured Like a Precious Jewel

Traditionally, the men considered it their solemn duty to protect and provide for the women in their family. They tolerated all kinds of hardships to ensure that the women and children had all the necessary comforts. Physically, a woman is more delicately built than a man. In addition, she tends to be more volatile emotionally. Thus, practically speaking, a woman needs physical protection as well as emotional support. Respecting these innate qualities of women, society was structured in such a way that it kept women under the secure umbrella of their family.

---

1. *Manu-smṛti* 3.56.

Nowadays, the notion of gender neutrality is becoming popular. The belief is that men and women are more or less identical but think or act differently only because of cultural conditioning. On these grounds, the women's liberation movement proposes doing away with the notion that women are the 'weaker sex' and need men as their protectors. Their conviction is that women don't have inherent feminine traits of being emotional or gentle and men don't have the inherent masculine traits of being rational or physically boisterous. They appear to be that way because that is what the society expects them to be, and if we were to train them differently, men would be as emotional as women and women as rational as men.

This concept of gender neutrality sparked the 'nature vs. nurture' debate on the origin of gender-based behaviors; in other words do men and women behave the way they do because of the biological differences they are born with, or due to their upbringing? It is generally accepted that both factors play a role in an individual's behavior, but the debate continues regarding which of the two is dominant. In either case, the Vedic understanding is that the 'nurturing' ought to be based on that which is given by 'nature.' It would be wise to consider that perhaps gender 'stereotypes' are an inherent part of cultures all over the world, not due to a perverse desire of men to exploit women, but because they take into consideration the biological and psychological makeup of men and women.

Śrīla Prabhupāda elaborates:

> A sixteen-year-old boy can go safely all over the world, but a sixteen-year girl cannot. That is not possible. By nature,

> they are weak. So they require protection. And until she reaches youthhood, she is protected by the father. As soon as she reaches youthhood, she is given to a young man, her husband, to give protection. And in old age, she is protected by the elderly sons. This is the Vedic culture.[1]

On the one hand, activists of the women's liberation movement claim that women are as strong as men and as capable of living independently, but on the other hand they are constantly petitioning for laws that give them protection. They rightly expect that women should be given protection, but instead of strengthening the family unit, they are expecting the state to step in and be the provider.

Śrīla Prabhupāda explains that Vedic culture advocates protection of women, and this was lovingly done by family members, just as one would be careful to protect something that is very precious and dear to them.

> Actually the woman must always be protected by her husband. We always speak of the goddess of fortune as being placed on the chest of Nārāyaṇa. In other words, the wife must remain embraced by her husband. Thus she becomes beloved and well protected. Just as one saves his money and places it under his own personal protection, one should similarly protect his wife by his own personal supervision. Just as intelligence is always within the heart, so a beloved chaste wife should always have her place on the chest of a good husband. This is the proper relationship between husband and wife. A wife is therefore called *ardhāṅganī*, or half of the body. One cannot remain

1. Lecture by Śrīla Prabhupāda, November 30, 1973.

> with only one leg, one hand or only one side of the body. He must have two sides.[1]

Such protection meant that the girls would not go anywhere unaccompanied. While it may seem restrictive to the point of being suffocating to modern women, traditional ladies were used to it and happy enough to potter around in their houses, going out only with other family members. Due to this, incidents of rape or harassment of women by strangers were practically unheard of. They were not subjected to the unpleasantness of outsiders 'checking them out' and making lewd remarks when they were outside their home, for the men accompanying them took seriously their responsibility of taking care of them, to the point of challenging anyone who even looked at them lustily.

Upholding a woman's dignity was a matter of utmost importance, and any violation was taken to be a poor reflection on the family and society itself. Along with the family members, the government was equally conscientious about protecting women. *Śrīmad-Bhāgavatam* describes that when one of the warrior princes, Arjuna, appeared to be morose and dejected, he was questioned by his elder brother, Yudhiṣṭhira: "You are always the protector of the deserving living beings, such as *brāhmaṇas* [priests and teachers], children, cows, women and the diseased. Could you not give them protection when they approached you for shelter? [...] Have you not properly treated a deserving woman?"[2] Śrīla Prabhupāda comments in the purport:

---

1. *Śrīmad-Bhāgavatam* 4.26.17, purport by Śrīla Prabhupāda.
2. *Śrīmad-Bhāgavatam* 1.14.42–43.

> The *brāhmaṇas,* who are always engaged in researching knowledge for the society's welfare work, both materially and spiritually, deserve the protection of the king in all respects. Similarly, the children of the state, the cow, the diseased person, the woman and the old man specifically require the protection of the state or a *kṣatriya* king. If such living beings do not get protection by the *kṣatriya,* or the royal order, or by the state, it is certainly shameful for the *kṣatriya* or the state. If such things had actually happened to Arjuna, Mahārāja Yudhiṣṭhira was anxious to know about these discrepancies.[1]

When I was newly married, I was taken aback when my in-laws would insist that, as far as possible, my husband, or one of them, accompany me whenever I had to go somewhere. My parents had been far more liberal in my upbringing. I had, alone, boarded the notorious Delhi buses umpteenth times, hitchhiked from our college campus to go to town, traveled overnight by train, and even flown to the remote northeastern state of Manipur when my father was posted there. So I felt I could easily handle a taxi ride from one location to another, and scoffed at the overprotective attitude of my in-laws.

But gradually, I began to appreciate that their primary concern was my safety. I was touched by the fact that they would work around their schedules just to ensure that they could be with me when I had to go half way across town for some work. This meant that I could not just pick up my bag at whim and leave the house whenever I wanted; I would have to discuss my plans with my family and wait for them to make suitable arrangements. But it was a minor inconvenience in exchange

1. *Śrīmad-Bhāgavatam* 1.14.42, purport by Śrīla Prabhupāda.

for being treated like a special person who should come to no harm. When I looked back, I remembered that my solitary trips had been peppered with several unpleasant incidents of groping. In fact, in retrospect many of those bold excursions seemed foolhardy, for it was just a matter of luck that nothing worse happened. It was a relief that I no longer had to be constantly on the alert for lecherous men.

Today, as a mother of two young girls, I'm no less protective towards them than my in-laws were with me twenty years ago. It's ironic that in this age when society's moral standards are at an all-time low, we encourage girls to travel alone. We would rather arm them with pepper sprays and self-defense training than stifle their independence by having a grown-up escort them. It's all very well to protest that every man should be perfectly self-controlled, but when every billboard and TV program is screaming the opposite, I'm not holding my breath that it will happen any time soon. In the meantime, even though we live in a safe rural community and my daughters are ten and fourteen years old, I drop them and pick them up from their dance classes, play dates, and after-school activities for I would rather be safe than sorry. Chaperoning has generally been abandoned as an outdated concept, but perhaps it's more needed today than a few generations ago when it was a common practice.

Protection, Not Subjugation

Protection and independence cannot go hand in hand. At the same time, this does not mean that the women should be micromanaged, with their every movement or action being controlled. Śrīla Prabhupāda elaborates:

> So according to Vedic system, there is no independent life for a woman. *Na strī svātantryam arhati. Manu-saṁhitā* states that "*strī*" – *strī* means woman – "should not be allowed independence." They should be given all protection. That's a very nice system. [...] Independence does not mean that their position is much lower, no. Just like children. Children have no independence. No independence means they are well-protected. No independence does not mean that he has no independence to act. No. He has got. But under the protection. Just like there are some nations known as protectorate. America is protecting. America is a big nation, and it is protecting another small nation. That does not mean that they have no independence. They are also independent. They are acting like that. But because they are weaker, they should be given protection.[1]

Thus, protection did not mean suppression of individuality. It meant providing a safe environment for women to thrive in.

However, gradually, with the onset of the age of consumerism, the rise of sense gratification and materialism has accompanied the decline in finer values of duty and honor. Protectors have become the oppressors. Particularly, as predicted by the scriptures, this is the age of quarrel and hypocrisy, so it is inevitable that some people misuse their authority to exploit their subordinates.

The women's liberation movement sought to correct such exploitation. Of course, any sane person would oppose evils such as domestic violence. In retrospect, however, it may be questioned whether the solution given by many women's

---

1. Lecture by Śrīla Prabhupāda, October 23, 1968. Edited. For original quote, see archived URL: http://bit.ly/SBLec

support groups has actually solved the problem or only served to add fuel to the fire. Their idea was to empower the women to walk out of their current unhappy situations and live independently. While this course of action may have helped temporarily in some cases where the situation was truly intolerable, it has had other, far more damaging repercussions which the feminists may not have bargained for.

Encouraging a woman to move out of her circle of protection puts her at the mercy of many other people who have no qualms about exploiting her, including the employer who helps her become 'independent' of her family by having an income of her own, but dependent instead on the source of that income, which in most cases happens to be a faceless organization that cares little for the welfare of the individual in its policy of maximizing profits. Since 2017, the participation of hundreds of women in the #MeToo movement on social media is a sad testimony to the widespread sexual harassment and assault that they face in the workplace. Although the main objective of the movement is to bring the perpetrators to task, it behooves us to consider the novel idea that perhaps women should not be forced into such precarious positions in the first place.

In Vedic culture, if the women were being mistreated, they could appeal to the elders in the family, who in turn would counsel the man in question and ensure that things were corrected. Instead of rejecting the model of protection within the family, actual reform should have focused on correcting such incidents of domestic abuse by instructing, educating and inspiring the men to rectify their behavior. At the same time, the women also need instruction, for 'it takes two to tango.' These days it is taboo to blame the victim – for good reason, because in many cases the women are helpless and at the receiving end of an unreasonable, violent spouse – but there are other cases where the two individuals are just rubbing each other the wrong way and a few adjustments in behavior on both sides could avert situations from escalating into unpleasantness of the worst kind.

It is a misconception that a patriarchal system inevitably means that women get the short end of the stick. These misconceptions are strengthened by horrifying phenomena such as female infanticide, dowry deaths and domestic violence towards women. Books like *The Breadwinner*[1] serve as a warning against the fanatical misapplication of protective principles, for it describes women who were so severely restricted under the Taliban rule in Afghanistan that they risked starvation if there was no male member in the house (because they were not allowed to step out alone even to buy basic provisions). But such dysfunctional behaviors were never part of Vedic culture, or any truly civilized system. These issues have cropped up as people moved further and further away from the high ideals which form the very basis of Vedic civilization. What we see today in most countries, is a warped form of the way things were earlier.

One proposed solution to fanatical interpretations of tradition is to undertake a complete overhaul and move away from traditional gender roles – but this is like throwing the baby out with the bath water. It would be more beneficial to establish the system the way it is meant to be, in its pristine form,

---

1. Deborah Ellis, *The Breadwinner*, (Toronto, Ontario: Groundwood Books, 2000).

where every individual is valued, first and foremost as a child of God, and every single life form — even animals, what to say of men, women, and children — lives a life free from fear. The men must take responsibility for properly giving protection and the women should graciously accept it.

Marriage

In every culture in the world, marriage is considered to be a ceremony of deep significance. In a Vedic wedding, a fire sacrifice is performed to worship the demigods and invite them to bear witness to the commitment undertaken by the bride and groom to remain by each other's side for the rest of their lives. However, over a period of time, many aspects of Vedic marriage have become distorted. As such, currently, misconceptions abound and the principles are largely misunderstood.

Early, Arranged Marriage: More Than a Marriage of Convenience

Much of what we perceive today as the norm are ideas fed to us consciously and subconsciously by the media (and after globalization took place, it is specifically the Western media who are the most vociferous). In the light of such 'norms,' the Vedic tradition of 'arranged marriage,' a phenomenon quite alien to today's Western society, is widely maligned by visions of young girls being forcibly married off to leering men old enough to be their grandfathers. Scholars, with little idea of the culture that goes along with the tradition of arranged marriages, denounce it as a violation of human rights. Stephanie Coontz, Director of Research and Public Education for the Council on Contemporary Families in the USA, writes:

> Many arranged marriages in many countries are associated with a lack of choice for young people and are particularly repressive to women. The fact that arranged marriages tend to be more stable is not a measure of success because we know that people are sometimes held in them without any options.[1]

Often, arranged marriages are wrongly equated with forced marriages and widely condemned. One would think that for most Westerners it's a foregone conclusion that a 'marriage of choice' or a 'love marriage' is a far superior alternative to an arranged marriage, yet the fact that the media goes out of its way to assert this conclusion either points to an underlying insecurity, or an arrogance that impels them to pass judgment without even understanding the nuances that make it work. A case in point is one portrayed in recent Disney movies. A recurring theme in many of them is that of the main female lead rejecting arranged marriage: the eponymous *Pocahontas* and *Mulan,* as well as Jasmine in *Aladdin* and Merida in *Brave,* to name a few. Writer Dani Colman notes:

---

1. Daniel Burke, "Does love last longer in arranged marriages?" *The Washington Post,* May 23, 2012, archived URL: http://bit.ly/LongLastLove

> Disney has, at this point, a very well-developed language of signifiers — many borrowed from the fairy tale culture Disney appropriates — for issues and themes too adult to actually show on the screen, and the best-known of these is marriage/betrothal/True Love's Kiss™ as a signifier for the consensual relationship between a man and a woman. Because of that, Disney has a pretty strict binary when it comes to marriage: arranged/non-consensual marriage = *bad*; consensual/love-predicated marriage—*good*. For a Disney princess, an arranged marriage is a fate worse than death: it is a loss of agency, a violation of consent, and, on a metaphorical level at least, a loss of ownership over her body.[1]

In each of the above mentioned movies, the chosen prospective spouse is depicted as someone stupid or mean, and in general completely unsuitable; the idea that someone should marry a person they are not in love with is clearly conveyed as ridiculous. However, according to the data collected by the Statistic Brain Research Institute in February 2018, more than 50% of marriages around the world are arranged but have a divorce rate of 6.3%. Considering this, it may be worthwhile to examine them further.[2]

In Vedic culture, marriage is a sacred union between two people. Similar to Christianity, in which the couple vows to stay together 'till death do us part,' there is no question of ending the relationship. The ceremony is performed with a fire sacrifice and is considered to be as irrevocable as birth

---

1. Dani Coleman, "Disney consents (or that damn troll scene)," *Medium*, February 4, 2014, archived URL: http://bit.ly/DisneyCon

2. Arranged/Forced Marriage Statistics, *Statistic Brain Research Institute*, April 10, 2018, archived URL: http://bit.ly/ArrMarry

or death. Because of the gravity of the vow, many factors are taken into consideration before entering into the alliance.

The parents carefully look for a suitable match for their child, often from families with a similar social and economic background. While this may be done partly to ensure that the children remain within their own community, it also automatically lays the groundwork for a smoother marriage since it ensures that both the boy and girl have grown up with similar values and customs. Determining compatibility using astrological calculations is another important factor which is almost always undertaken. In the right hands, Vedic astrology is an advanced, ancient science of calculating the mental, emotional, intellectual and sexual matching of the couple. Apart from this, the parents talk to common acquaintances and try to gather as much information as they can about the family and the prospective spouse before making the final decision. In previous ages, the bride and groom would not even see each other before they got married. Although this may seem unreal to today's independent-minded young people, it was quite acceptable for children who had complete trust that their parents were looking out for their best interests and, in their wisdom, would pick the most suitable spouse for them. Respect for elders was a very prominent part of Vedic culture, and young boys and girls willingly accepted their decision when it came to important things such as marriage, starting a business, or buying property.

Vedic culture places a high value on purity — in both men and women. The analogy of butter invariably melting in the presence of fire is used to describe the interaction between a man and a woman, and one is warned not to underestimate the sexual urge. The understanding is that sexual tension between people is inevitable, but to be cultured means not to aggravate it. This, in fact, is explained to be one of the characteristics that distinguish men from animals — the restraint of base urges for the sake of achieving a higher consciousness. As such, the society was organized to prevent frivolous mixing between men and women. This was one of the reasons that the arranged marriage system was an essential part of Vedic culture, for there was no question of young girls dating men, or entering into relationships to try and see whether it works, casually losing their virginity in the process.

Another reason for parents' intervention was the consideration that a young person often lacks the maturity and discrimination to make this important decision for himself or herself. This was particularly true earlier, when children were married at a much younger age, but even now, the kind of foresight a middle-aged person has cannot be compared to that of one in his twenties. Such astuteness on the part of the elders particularly has its place in the Vedic marriage, for the basis of such a marriage is not sexual attraction. This is the real paradigm shift and the answer to those who question the idea of marrying a person with whom one is not in love.

The aim of marriage in Vedic culture is for the husband and wife to help each other advance spiritually. Actually, this is considered to be the aim of life itself and therefore everything — marriage, education and work — is naturally designed to help fulfill this goal. What this means, in simple terms, is that while it is acknowledged that there is attraction between men and women, it is not considered to be the be all and end all of life. Love and affection are expected to develop naturally between individuals when they are performing their duty as enjoined by scriptures, and serving each other as husband and wife. The emphasis is on maintaining high ideals of humility, service, truthfulness, kindness, and cleanliness.

The husband and wife enter into marriage secure in the knowledge that this is the person who is going to be by their side throughout their life and together they will progress towards the higher goal of developing love for God; they are grateful for each other's support and happily do their part in maintaining harmony in the family. This, then, is the real reason for marriage in Vedic culture, and having the elders of the family arrange the match is the natural way to go about it. From the word go, the couple know their duty and do not have unreal expectations of being 'swept off their feet.' At the same time, it does not mean that the people involved are devoid of emotions and go through married life as if it were a business transaction. As happens in most cases, over a period of time profound love develops between the couple, particularly in cases when they are married young and their partner provides their first and only exposure to a relationship with the opposite sex.

Śrīla Prabhupāda elaborates:

> Today in Hindu society, unmarried girls are still taught to worship Lord Śiva with the idea that they may get husbands like him. Lord Śiva is the ideal husband, not in the sense of riches or sense gratification, but because he is the greatest of all devotees. [...] The girls are not taught to select a husband who is very rich or very opulent for material sense gratification; rather, if a girl is fortunate enough to get a husband as good as Lord Śiva in devotional service, then her life becomes perfect. The wife is dependent on the husband, and if the husband is a Vaiṣṇava [devotee], then

> naturally she shares the devotional service of the husband because she renders him service. This reciprocation of service and love between husband and wife is the ideal of a householder's life.[1]

Śrīmad-Bhāgavatam narrates the history of princess Devahūti, the daughter of Emperor Svāyambhuva Manu. She was endowed with all good qualities, and was so beautiful that a demigod traveling in the sky became so enchanted on seeing her playing with a ball on the palace terrace that he fell headlong from his airplane. On hearing from the saint Nārada Muni about the exalted character of a sage l iving in the forest named Kardama Muni, Devahūti became attracted to him and expressed her desire to marry him. Her parents approved and immediately set off to look for Kardama Muni.

Śrīla Prabhupāda comments in this context:

> The girl Devahūti did not personally see Kardama Muni, nor did she personally experience his character or qualities, since there was no social intercourse by which she could gain such understanding. But she heard about Kardama Muni from the authority of Nārada Muni. Hearing from an authority is a better experience than gaining personal understanding. She heard from Nārada Muni that Kardama Muni was just fit to be her husband; therefore she became fixed in her heart that she would marry him, and she expressed her desire to her father, who therefore brought her before him.[2]
>
> The selection of a good husband for a good girl was always entrusted to the parents. Here it is clearly stated that Manu

1. *Śrīmad-Bhāgavatam* 3.23.1, purport by Śrīla Prabhupāda.
2. *Śrīmad-Bhāgavatam* 3.22.10, purport by Śrīla Prabhupāda.

> and his wife were coming to see Kardama Muni to offer their daughter because the daughter was well qualified and the parents were searching out a similarly qualified man. This is the duty of parents. Girls are never thrown into the public street to search out their husband, for when girls are grown up and are searching after a boy, they forget to consider whether the boy they select is actually suitable for them. Out of the urge of sex desire, a girl may accept anyone, but if the husband is chosen by the parents, they can consider who is to be selected and who is not. According to the Vedic system, therefore, the girl is given over to a suitable boy by the parents; she is never allowed to select her own husband independently.[1]

The marriages were arranged by the parents, but this did not mean that the girl had no say in the matter. Particularly, a royal princess would have a ceremony called *svayaṁvara,* in which qualified men would line up, and she had the liberty of selecting one whom she considered suitable.

Marriage was considered to be an integral part of a woman's life. While a man may remain celibate all his life, every woman was expected to be married so that she is sheltered and secure amidst her husband, children, and grandchildren. At the present time, particularly in the Western countries, a number of women are choosing to remain single, yet many regret their decision when they advance in age and are beset with loneliness. Feminist Lori Gottlieb, in her article entitled *Marry Him! The case for settling for Mr. Good Enough,* reveals:

> Of course, we'd be loath to admit it in this day and age, but ask any soul-baring 40-year-old single heterosexual woman

1. *Śrīmad-Bhāgavatam* 3.21.27, purport by Śrīla Prabhupāda.

> what she most longs for in life, and she probably won't tell you it's a better career or a smaller waistline or a bigger apartment. Most likely, she'll say that what she really wants is a husband (and, by extension, a child). To the outside world, of course, we still call ourselves feminists and insist — vehemently, even — that we're independent and self-sufficient and don't believe in any of that damsel-in-distress stuff, but in reality, we aren't fish who can do without a bicycle, we're women who want a traditional family. And despite growing up in an era when the centuries-old mantra to get married young was finally (and, it seemed, refreshingly) replaced by encouragement to postpone that milestone in pursuit of high ideals (education! career! but also true love!), every woman I know — no matter how successful and ambitious, how financially and emotionally secure — feels panic, occasionally coupled with desperation, if she hits 30 and finds herself unmarried.[1]

While anticipating feminist backlash for her comments, she states that anyone who claims to not be worried about being single and above thirty is either in denial or is lying. She says vehemently:

> My advice is this: Settle! That's right. Don't worry about passion or intense connection. Don't nix a guy based on his annoying habit of yelling "Bravo!" in movie theaters. Overlook his halitosis or abysmal sense of aesthetics. Because if you want to have the infrastructure in place to have a family, settling is the way to go. Based on my observations, in fact, settling will probably make you happier in the long run, since many of those who marry

1. Lori Gottlieb, "Marry Him! The case for settling for Mr. Good Enough," *The Atlantic*, March 2008, archived URL: http://bit.ly/atlanticmarry

with great expectations become more disillusioned with each passing year.

Not only was it recommended that women get married, it was also expected that they marry while they are young. Child marriages have now been banned because the custom persisted without the underlying culture that goes with it. Earlier, children were married as young as five years old, but the girls would continue to live with their parents till they came of age. Then they would go and live with their husband. At that time, at the tender age of twelve or thirteen, she would still be treated as a child, allowed to play with other girls in the neighborhood, swing in the courtyard, go to carnivals with other family members and so on, and would be expected to be a helping hand to the elder ladies in the house, much as she would help her mother in her parents' house. Gradually, she would be given more and more responsibility in the house. As a result, just as the girl had a strong bond with her own family, she would develop deep relationships with the members of her husband's family, because a significant part of her childhood would have been spent in their house and she would have experienced reciprocation of service and care.

Unfortunately, with deterioration of culture and high ideals among common folk, there were cases of the husband's family simply using the child as unpaid household help, and trying to exploit her by expecting her to serve them hand and foot, while they on their part did not take care of her as one would a young child. In addition, the breakdown of the joint family led to the unrealistic situation of young girls getting married and immediately having to handle the load of managing a complete household by themselves. There were also other unfortunate incidents where the parents overburdened by too many daughters hastily married them to unsuitable men who were sometimes many, many years older than them. Such incidents eventually led to the abolition of child marriage.

Nevertheless, the reasoning behind early marriage is the understanding that one experiences attraction for the opposite sex fairly early in life. It is hypocritical to allow children as young as ten or twelve years old to date, thereby implicitly allowing them to be physically intimate, but at the same time being appalled at cultures in which children are married at that age so that the relationship is not illicit. In the West, it is still considered scandalous for unmarried girls in their early teens to have babies (unfortunately, such opprobrium nourishes the flourishing abortion industry). But many Westerners consider it an even greater scandal when girls in their early teens get married before becoming pregnant. The idea is so repugnant to them that they establish non-profit organizations dedicated to 'rescuing' young girls in other countries from arranged marriages at a young age. They appear much more comfortable with the idea of girls getting pregnant prior to marriage or having abortions.

Now in India, child marriage, which previously was an intrinsic part of the culture, is literally a crime. Indian law bizarrely prohibits marriage for females before age eighteen, and for males before twenty-one, yet allows consensual sex from age sixteen. Hence it is legal for a sixteen-year-old girl to have sex and become pregnant, but illegal for her to marry!

While the legitimization of marriage by choice may technically give a lady the freedom to choose whom she wants to marry, it essentially means that she has to wait for someone to fall in love with her. She's forced to enter the dating game, whether she likes it or not, entering into a series of relationships while waiting to meet 'the one,' which entails much heartache and pressure to be physically attractive to the opposite sex. The feminists tried to resolve this problem by undermining the institution of marriage itself and encouraging women to remain single, but that in turn has put more pressure on women, who now have to manage their households, jobs, children and health — all by themselves.

Śrīla Prabhupāda summarizes the Vedic principle of early, arranged marriage:

> In Vedic society no girl was allowed to remain independent and unmarried. Independence for women means they become like prostitutes, struggling to capture some man who will take care of her. In this way, the so-called independent woman has to work very hard to make herself attractive by artificially wearing cosmetics, mini-skirts, and so many other things. Formerly, the girl would be married to a suitable boy at a very early age, say six years old. Although a girl was married early she did not stay with her husband immediately, but was gradually trained in so many ways on how to cook, clean, and serve her husband — up until the time of her puberty. So all the time there was no anxiety because a girl would know "I have got a husband" and the boy would know "I have got this girl as my wife." Therefore, when the boy and girl would come of age, there was no chance of illicit sex-life. And the psychology is that the first boy that a girl accepts in marriage, he's the one she will completely give her heart to, and this attachment on the girl's side for her husband becomes stronger and stronger. Thus, if a girl gets a good husband — one who has accepted a bona fide spiritual master and is firmly fixed up in his service — automatically

> the wife of such a good husband inherits all the benefits of his spiritual advancement.[1]

When my husband and I were living abroad, we employed a mature lady from India to give me a helping hand at home with the children. Within a few weeks, she was completely distraught and was demanding to be sent back home. She said that her husband had fallen ill because of missing her intensely, and she too was finding it very difficult to live without him. I found it quite surprising that, despite being middle-aged, the husband and wife were acting so sentimentally towards each other, willing to give up a source of income which they clearly needed just so they could be together. But our nanny explained that she had gotten married at a very young age, and that she and her husband had literally grown up together. So practically all their lives they had been by each other's side, and they just didn't know how to manage otherwise. I was struck by the simplicity and sweetness of this couple's affection for each other. I could see how strong a girl's attachment for her husband would be, if he is the only man she has known intimately and she marries him while she's still quite young.

Today, men and women like to 'play the field' before settling down. Although ostensibly this is done to ensure that they end up with the person they are most compatible with, the previous relationships leave an indelible mark on one's consciousness, particularly for the woman, since she is likely to get more emotionally involved. It may also have an impact on her marriage, because she may end up unfavorably comparing her husband's temperament with that of an ex-boyfriend, not

---

1. Letter by Śrīla Prabhupāda to Naiṣkarmī written from Bhaktivedanta Manor, UK, 28 Jul 1973. Edited. For original quote, see archived URL: http://bit.ly/Vanisource

realizing that the husband's occasional outbursts of irritation may be due to juggling far more responsibilities than her ever-cheerful boyfriend who had refused to make a serious commitment.

For the principle of early marriage to work, many factors have to work in tandem. The parents of the girl and the boy should spend adequate time in investigating whether they are suitable for each other. Also, they should be available to give physical and moral support to the young couple. The boy and girl, even though married young, should comprehend and accept the gravity of their vow, and should have a proper understanding of their respective roles. They should be willing to grow with their spouse, rather than grow apart if there are changes in their attitude and character as they age.

Without all these dynamics in place, even the most well-meaning attempt to revive child marriage is doomed to fail. But at least we can begin to apply the principle by emphasizing to young people the advantages of marrying early and encouraging them not to wait till they are in their late twenties or thirties to get married. Also, we should avoid indiscriminately denouncing cultures where girls are married at a young age.

Dowry: A Girl's Rightful Inheritance

Dowry refers to gifts given by the girl's parents to the newlyweds at the time of her marriage. *Śrīmad-Bhāgavatam* describes that "Empress Śatarūpā [Devahūti's mother] lovingly gave most valuable presents, suitable for the occasion, such as jewelry, clothes and household articles, in dowry to the bride and bridegroom."[1] Śrīla Prabhupāda comments:

1. *Śrīmad-Bhāgavatam* 3.22.23.

> In the Vedic way of marriage such a dowry is still given to the bridegroom by the father of the bride; even in poverty-stricken India there are marriages where hundreds and thousands of rupees are spent for a dowry. The dowry system is not illegal, as some have tried to prove. The dowry is a gift given to the daughter by the father to show good will, and it is compulsory. In rare cases where the father is completely unable to give a dowry, it is enjoined that he must at least give a fruit and a flower. As stated in *Bhagavad-gītā,* God can also be pleased even by a fruit and a flower. When there is financial inability and no question of accumulating a dowry by another means, one can give a fruit and flower for the satisfaction of the bridegroom.[1]

Unfortunately, in more recent times, there have been numerous cases where this system has been misused by the groom's family to put undue pressure on the bride's side, and make unreasonable demands on what they expect the dowry to be. The issue took a particularly nasty turn when some truly demoniac families burnt their young daughters-in-law to death because of being dissatisfied with the dowry given by their parents.[2] However, as explained above, originally, dowry was given "according to the position of the father of

1. *Śrīmad-Bhāgavatam* 3.22.23, purport by Śrīla Prabhupāda.

2. In 1961, laws were enforced to prevent such atrocities. Section 498A of the Indian Penal Code requires the bridegroom and his family to be automatically arrested if a wife complains of dowry harassment. Unfortunately, the flip side of the coin is that the law has been widely abused by unscrupulous women to get their husband's family in trouble by falsely framing them and then demanding a monetary settlement in exchange for dropping the charges against them. To prevent this, in 2014, the Supreme Court ruled that arrests can only be made with a magistrate's approval.

the bride."[1] There would be no explicit list of demands given by the groom's family, nor a price quoted as if the boy were up for sale. It was given out of affection for their daughter, and also to help the newlyweds set up their house.

Giving a dowry was an important part of the patriarchal system, for it allowed the parents to be equal towards their children, be they sons or daughters. The sons would get the property and wealth after the father becomes old or leaves his body, but most of the daughter's share was given at the time of her marriage and later also, as gifts whenever she would visit her parents' house, or if they would visit her. This is the reason "hundreds of thousands of rupees are spent," for it is considered to be her rightful share.

Polygamy: For Protection, Not Frivolous Enjoyment

Vedic marriages were traditionally polygamous. Although there are isolated cases of polyandrous marriages — the most famous being that of Draupadī marrying the five Pāṇḍava princes as described in the historical epic, *Mahābhārata* — the most common form was polygyny. Men acting as the protectors were allowed to take on the responsibility of having more than one wife, but there was no justifiable reason for a woman to have more than one husband.

A person from a society that has only monogamous marriages might imagine polygamy to be sinful, for it appears to encourage lusty men to legally enjoy intimate relations with a large number of women. Factually, in the Vedic tradition, although polygamy was allowed, it did not mean that every

1. *Śrīmad-Bhāgavatam* 3.22.23, purport by Śrīla Prabhupāda.

man would have a 'harem' of twenty, thirty women to himself, simply because most men could not afford it since accepting a woman in marriage meant that he would take complete responsibility for her. The decision to have more than one wife was taken in the spirit of accepting the obligation of protecting the women of the community, particularly in situations when women outnumbered men in society, rather than with an idea of irresponsibly reveling in the company of a large number of sexual partners. Each of the co-wives and her children were properly taken care of.

Śrīla Prabhupāda explains the principle of polygamy (more precisely, polygyny).

> Generally in every society the female population is greater in number than the male population. Therefore if it is a principle in the society that all girls should be married, unless polygamy is allowed it will not be possible. If all the girls are not married there is a good chance of adultery, and a society in which adultery is allowed cannot be very peaceful or pure.[1]

> People have become so degraded in this age that on the one hand they restrict polygamy and on the other hand they hunt for women in so many ways. Many business concerns publicly advertise that topless girls are available in this club or in that shop. Thus women have become instruments of sense enjoyment in modern society. The *Vedas* enjoin, however, that if a man has the propensity to enjoy more than one wife — as is sometimes the propensity for men in the higher social order, such as the *brāhmaṇas, kṣatriyas*, and *vaiśyas*, and even sometimes the *śūdras* — he

1. *Śrī Caitanya-caritāmṛta* 1.14.58, purport by Śrīla Prabhupāda.

> is allowed to marry more than one wife. Marriage means taking complete charge of a woman and living peacefully without debauchery. At the present moment, however, debauchery is unrestricted. Nonetheless, society makes a law that one should not marry more than one wife. This is typical of a demoniac society.[1]

In his article *Are People "Naturally" Polygamous?* psychologist Michael E. Price points out:

> [A]lthough Western culture remains officially monogamous, it tolerates de facto polygamy in many forms. For example, serial monogamists like Donald Trump and Larry King divorce older wives to marry younger ones, which serves to monopolize the fertile years of multiple women (the same thing that polygamy would accomplish). Celebrities like Hugh Hefner and Charlie Sheen live openly with multiple girlfriends, and various male athletes, rock stars, and actors accumulate hundreds or thousands of sexual partners.[2]

Although it is generally supposed that women do not like the idea of having to share their husband with co-wives, for some it may be an attractive proposition. For example, if given a choice between having all to one's self a husband who is an ordinary clerk or of being a co-wife of a wealthy celebrity, many women would prefer the latter. And factually, polygamy has traditionally been practiced mostly by men of above-average means. Price supports this idea:

---

1. *Śrīmad-Bhāgavatam* 4.26.6, purport by Śrīla Prabhupāda.
2. Michael E. Price, "Are People "Naturally" Polygamous? The human mind evolved in a polygamous world," *Psychology Today,* August 18, 2011, archived URL: http://bit.ly/Psychtoday1

> Most ancestral men aspired to polygyny, even if only a minority could achieve it, while many ancestral women perceived that their own interests would be better served as the co-wife of a really impressive man than as the sole wife of a lesser one. [...] That's why there is so much de facto polygyny in Western culture, despite the West's attempts to abolish polygyny in favor of a marriage system that biologist Richard Alexander refers to as "socially imposed monogamy."

Apart from economic and social benefits that a woman may derive from such a marriage, *Encyclopedia Britannica* also lists some health benefits:

> Polygyny can also have a positive effect on maternal and child health. During postpartum recovery, for instance, co-wives can usually rely upon each other to perform the most strenuous work of the household. By creating opportunities for sexual companionship among the other members of the marriage, polygyny also supports the once common expectation that women will remain sexually abstinent for two or more years during and after pregnancy. This practice fosters adequate birth spacing for the mother to recover from the physiological and emotional stresses associated with pregnancy, lactation, and the care of a young child.[1]

Certainly there may be jealousy or rivalry among co-wives, but it was expected and taken in their stride, just as traditionally there would sometimes be friction between the mother-in-law and daughter-in-law. Generally, girls were trained to live

1. The editors of Encyclopaedia Britannica. "Polygyny, Marriage," In *Encyclopaedia Britannica*, June 30, 2018, archived URL: http://bit.ly/britpolygyny

peacefully with the co-wives of their husband, treating each other like sisters, being respectful to those who were older than them and affectionate to those who were younger.

The *Mahābhārata* describes that when Arjuna, one of the five husbands of Draupadī, married Subhadrā, she was naturally fearful of Draupadī's reaction. When they reached the palace, Subhadrā dressed herself very simply, and upon meeting Draupadī knelt down at her feet and said, "I am your maidservant." Charmed by her humility, Draupadī immediately embraced her and happily welcomed her into the household.

The Vedic scriptures also warn of the disastrous effects when co-wives' rivalry gets out of hand. King Daśaratha's wife Kaikeyī demanded that her senior co-wife's son Rāma be banished to the forest and her son Bharata be appointed heir apparent (*Rāmāyaṇa*), and King Citraketu's wives plotted to poison the only son of the senior-most co-wife (*Śrīmad-Bhāgavatam*, Canto 6). In each of the situations, the ladies in question later deeply repented their terrible actions.

As a family institution, polygamy has further benefits. As in the joint family, polygamy provides a support system for women and children. It also provides the means and facility for all women in the society to physically and legitimately become mothers, and subsequently for them and their children to be maintained and protected.

Instead of presenting polygyny as an institution which serves to belittle women, the Vedic view implies that a man's desire for several wives indicates how much he values the positive contribution of women in his life. Śrīla Prabhupāda states the following in the context of *kṣatriyas,* the royal administrative class.

> *Kṣatriyas* and *gṛhasthas* [householders] [...] actually need the encouragement of their wives in order to execute their duties. Indeed, a *gṛhastha* or *kṣatriya* cannot properly execute his responsibilities without the association of his wife. [...] *Kṣatriyas* were even allowed to have many wives to encourage them in discharging the duties of government. The association of a good wife is necessary in a life of *karma* and political affairs.[1]

Polygamy was traditionally well-accepted in Hinduism, Buddhism, and Islam. And even some Christians contest that the insistence on monogamy is not supported by their scriptures; indeed, the Old Testament clearly mentions instances of polygamy. But although polygamy is an ancient and very practical feature of human civilization, due to the influence of modern Christian morality, it has greatly declined throughout the world.

Just as an early, arranged marriage requires an entire cultural background for it to work, similarly the principle of polygamy will be successful only when certain conditions are met. The men who accept more than one wife should be prepared to support each of them properly. They should not enter into the alliance with a spirit of enjoyment. Rather, their intention should be to provide protection to the women of their community. The women, too, need to have a proper understanding of how to function in such a set-up. They should be humble like Subhadrā and not be solely focused on their

1. *Śrīmad-Bhāgavatam* 5.1.29, purport by Śrīla Prabhupāda.

own needs, for then they may end up like the vicious, envious wives of Citraketu.

In modern society, it is hard to find such noble-minded people. When people are struggling to even maintain a monogamous marriage, it would be impractical to try and institute polygamy, unless we first create the ideal culture and raise the consciousness of the individuals involved. It is certainly not advisable to practice polygamy in countries where it is illegal.

However, despite the fact that it is currently infeasible to implement polygamy, we should still be able to appreciate the advantages that it offers, and understand why it was an essential part of Vedic culture. There are still some parts of the world, such as the Middle Eastern countries, where polygamy is prevalent and unless we have proof to the contrary, we should not automatically assume that the women there are being mistreated because of it.

Stable Marriages, No Divorce

There is no such thing as divorce in Vedic culture. In fact, the word doesn't exist in the ancient language, Sanskrit, nor even in contemporary Indian languages such as Hindi. Radical as it may sound, in most cases there were no grounds for divorce in Vedic marriages. To begin with, the husband and wife had a high chance of being compatible, for the arranged marriage system ensured that the couple had similar background, upbringing and values. Even if there were minor incompatibilities, they were overlooked because people getting married understood that it was a commitment for life. This acceptance had a profound influence on the overall stability of married life. The wife tolerated the wet towels left on the floor by the husband, or him being irritable after a harrowing day at work, and similarly, the husband would not be seriously disturbed by the wife's nagging, or the fact that she's not as thin and smooth-skinned as she was a decade ago when they married.

One may think that predetermined stability would make people complacent and unwilling to make much of an effort in the relationship, for there is no threat of it falling apart. But this was not the case because in the Vedic system individuals were educated to perform their duty diligently, and by seeing the example of their own parents the children understood how this would result in a peaceful and happy family life. This is the reverse of the vicious cycle that children of divorced parents are subjected to; studies show that children whose parents have divorced are more likely to divorce — for they see it as a valid alternative to difficulties in marriage. One who is ingrained with a sense of duty and loyalty towards his family does not need the threat of divorce to treat his spouse well.

The lack of willingness to consider the option of divorce particularly helped the marriage when faced with more challenging circumstances, such as health crises, losing a child, or financial difficulties; the couple stood by each other and that, in fact, helped strengthen the marriage for they were grateful for each other's support. Just like children do not consider giving up the company of their parents or siblings even if they fall upon hard times, for the relationship is considered to be irrevocable, similarly, there was no question of the wife abandoning her husband if he lost all his money, or the husband leaving his wife if she were diagnosed with cancer.

Śrīla Prabhupāda narrates an incident in this regard. In the 1930s, in Bombay, he saw a beggar who was sitting on the roadside. The beggar was blind and his face was disfigured. But Prabhupāda noticed that he was neat and clean, and that sitting beside him was his young wife, who was similarly neat and clean. Prabhupāda could understand that somehow or other, due to some accident the man's face had become disfigured and he had lost his sight. Now, just to make a living he had to resort to begging. He was ugly and completely broke, yet despite all this, his wife had not abandoned him. She had taken it upon herself to look after him, keep him presentable, take him home at the end of the day and bring him back the next day. Śrīla Prabhupāda was impressed by the lady's faithfulness and devotion towards her husband.[1]

There are numerous examples in the scriptures of wives who have similarly not forsaken their husbands even when they have lost all their wealth and prestige. Princess Sītā accompanied Prince Rāma to the forest when he was banished, disregarding the royal comforts of the palace in favor of being by her husband's side (*Rāmāyaṇa*). Likewise, Draupadī went with her husbands to the forest when they were cheated out of their inheritance by their cousins (*Mahābhārata*).

Similarly, Vedic scriptures also give examples of husbands who have been tolerant of their wife's bad behavior. King Daśaratha's wife sent his favorite son to the forest for fourteen years which left him so heartbroken that it ultimately led to

1. Lecture by Śrīla Prabhupāda, July 28, 1973.

his death, and King Citraketu's wives poisoned his only son, but neither of them divorced their wives or left them to fend for themselves.

Fascinated by the overall stability of arranged marriages, Dr. Robert Epstein, a Ph.D. graduate in psychology from Harvard University and former editor in chief of *Psychology Today,* conducted research to better understand the system and learn lessons from it which may be applied to improve marriages in the West (which have a dismally high divorce rate). For the past fifteen years, he has interviewed more than a hundred couples in arranged marriages, from diverse backgrounds such as Indian, Pakistani and Orthodox Jewish.

In his research paper, Dr. Epstein states that his findings correlate with previous research: feelings of love in love matches begin to fade by as much as 50% within the first eighteen months, whereas perception of love in the arranged marriages tends to grow gradually, surpassing the love in the unarranged marriages at about the five-year mark. Within ten years, the affection felt by those in arranged marriages is typically twice as strong. One reason for this phenomenon, he claims, is that people in cultures where arranged marriage is practiced perceive love to be a deep emotion that develops over a period of time. In contrast, people in autonomous marriages, influenced by Hollywood movies, often confuse lust for love and are disappointed when the physical attraction begins to fade.

Śrīla Prabhupāda stated that to love means to have a desire to please the person we love, by serving him or her. He says,

> Love means *bhajanti*, render service. That is love. That is the beginning of love. So even if there is no love, if you,

> under the prescribed rules and regulation — if you simply render service, then you will develop love.[1]

He explains that if we love someone, we would actively like to do something to make them happy, and when the other person similarly reciprocates, the emotions become stronger. On the other hand, when we are simply thinking of enjoying our senses, that is lust.

Thus, in a Vedic marriage the wife serves the husband by cooking for him, looking after the children and other family members, and handling the housework, and he in turn is attentive to her needs, and protects and provides for her. In this way, there is reciprocation of service and their affection for each other increases. Their commitment is strong and there is no danger of 'falling out of love' for their love is not a frivolous or fleeting emotion. It is based on sacrifice and respect for each other.

Dr. Epstein blames the myths propagated by cultural mythmakers such as The Walt Disney Company for contributing to the "failure of many marriages around the world."[2] American women generally maintain this notion of romantic love, by which they think they will meet the 'man of their dreams,' marry and live happily ever after. In reality, when these starry-eyed ladies get married and have to face the day-to-day problems of life, or the bickering that is almost inevitable between husband and wife, they are disappointed and somewhat unprepared because they expected that 'love conquers all.' At this point, considering that they have made a mistake about their choice

1. Lecture by Śrīla Prabhupāda, December 19, 1966.

2. Robert Epstein, "How Walt Disney Ruined Our Love Lives. The myth of 'happily ever after'," *Brandeis Magazine,* Summer 2014, archived URL: http://bit.ly/Brandisney

of 'true love,' many women end their marriage and think about trying again. According to Dr. Epstein:

> We are bombarded daily by unrealistic messages about love and marriage — messages that make us think about leaving a relationship the moment our romantic expectations are dashed. As a result, nearly half of first marriages in the U.S. end in divorce. So do two-thirds of second marriages and three-quarters of third marriages.

In this context, Reva Seth, a Canadian journalist and author of *First Comes Marriage: Modern Relationship Advice from the Wisdom of Arranged Marriages,* opines:

> By their very nature (and the way they come together), arranged marriages don't fit into any of [the] models or narratives of romance shown in advertising and popular culture. It's not about finding your soulmate, or having Mr. Right conveniently stumble into your life. Instead, arranged marriages are about taking a practical approach to finding a life partner based on shared values and goals.[1]

Seth, who interviewed more than 300 women in arranged marriages, found that they are usually determined to make it work and are more likely to focus on positive aspects of their relationship. Contrasting the attitude of women in arranged marriages with that of the average Western woman, she says:

> In this part of the world, even in committed relationships, we're constantly asking ourselves: Could I do better? Would someone else make me happier? That kind of mentality — coupled with how easy it is, legally and socially, to get

1. Reva Seth, "Post Valentines Day: Rewrite Romance Arranged Marriage Style," *HuffPost Life*, March 18, 2009, archived URL: http://bit.ly/huffvalentine

> divorced – makes it extremely difficult to duplicate the level of commitment that I found among the women I spoke with.[1]

Another important feature that contributed to the stability of a Vedic marriage was that spouses' basic approach towards life and issues such as raising children, maintaining a particular standard of living and attitude towards family members were likely to be similar, not only because of similar cultural and social backgrounds, but because at that time everyone accepted the Vedic scriptures as guidebooks on how to lead their lives. Because these valuable texts are remarkably consistent and contain a wealth of knowledge, they helped people remain grounded. Women aspired to be like the exemplary Devahūti, and men like her worthy husband, Kardama Muni (*Śrīmad-Bhāgavatam*, Canto 3). In addition, the prevalence of traditional gender roles meant that the men and women clearly knew what their duties were in the household, which resulted in a harmonious marriage. The lady was secure in the knowledge that her husband would do his best to provide for the family and the husband was assured that his wife was handling the home front and taking care of the children.

Despite all the checks and balances, there may be an unfortunate situation where a woman is married to a person who doesn't follow the instructions of the scriptures, and instead of protecting her, mistreats and abuses her. What is a woman to do if there is no divorce? In Vedic culture, if indeed the marriage was considered to be beyond repair, and no amount of good counsel from the elders would make the husband change his bad ways, the husband and wife would separate.

1. Maura Kelly, "What's so Crazy About an Arranged Marriage?" *The Atlantic*, May 1, 2012, archived URL: http://bit.ly/atlanticrazy

The wife would return back to her parents' house, and live under the protection of her father or elder brother. However, this did not imply that the marriage itself was reversed or annulled, and that she could marry again. She would accept that marriage was not meant to be for her and spend the rest of her life living modestly, raising her children and being engaged in godly activities.

In the section of *Śrīmad-Bhāgavatam* that describes the activities and qualities of an ideal woman, particularly emphasizing her duty to serve her husband, Śrīla Prabhupāda comments:

> It is not that a chaste woman should be like a slave while her husband is *narādhama,* the lowest of men. Although the duties of a woman are different from those of a man, a chaste woman is not meant to serve a fallen husband. If her husband is fallen, it is recommended that she give up his association. Giving up the association of her husband does not mean, however, that a woman should marry again and thus indulge in prostitution. If a chaste woman unfortunately marries a husband who is fallen, she should live separately from him.[1]

This may seem unfair. Granted that she is allowed to separate and avoid the abuse, but why would she not be allowed to remarry? Again, to understand this concept better, one needs to appreciate the values that were an inseparable part of Vedic culture. The main idea is not to 'eat, drink, and be merry for tomorrow we die.' People accepted that everything happened according to God's will, so while they would do their part to have a materially comfortable life, if misfortune fell upon them despite their efforts, they would not break their heads trying to

1. *Śrīmad-Bhāgavatam* 7.11.28, purport by Śrīla Prabhupāda.

reverse it. Therefore, if a lady ended up with a terrible husband, and she left his house to live separately, she would not just jump right back in the dating scene to meet someone else to fall in love with. She would, instead, seize her unfortunate circumstances as an opportunity to be more God-conscious and engage in devotional activities. It was considered far more important to maintain the sanctity of marriage rather than give a second (or third, fourth, or fifth) chance to someone whose marriage had failed.

In actuality, opening the door to divorce with the intention to benefit the victims of abuse has led to the breakdown of even those marriages where the conflict is not so extreme. An online divorce service in the UK records 'Unreasonable Behavior' as one of the grounds for getting a divorce. The website goes on to explain:

> In an unreasonable behaviour petition, the petitioner sets out a number of allegations against the respondent. These allegations might include references to excessive drinking or financial extravagance, for example; but it's worth bearing in mind that the court doesn't insist on really severe allegations of unreasonable behaviour in order to grant a divorce. Relatively mild allegations such as devoting too much time to a career, having no common interests or pursuing a separate social life may well suffice.[1]

In Vedic culture, women, children and old men are particularly treated with care, so certainly it was allowed for a lady to walk away from a situation of severe abuse or torture within the marriage. However, it would be unthinkable for her to end

1. The Grounds for Divorce in England and Wales, *DivorceOnline,* June 30, 2018, archived URL: http://bit.ly/divorceng

her sacred vow because her husband is 'devoting too much time to a career' or has 'no common interests' with her! Mild misunderstandings between husband and wife were considered normal and not taken seriously. Śrīla Prabhupāda quoted the following Sanskrit saying:

ajā-yuddhe muni-śrāddhe
prabhāte megha-ḍambare
dāmpatya-kalahe caiva
bahv-ārambhe laghu-kriyā

Four things are to be considered insignificant — the fighting of goats, a ceremony observed by some sages in the forest, a thundering cloud in the morning and a quarrel between husband and wife. Śrīla Prabhupāda explains that goats may appear to be locking horns very fiercely, but the minute someone comes along and claps his hands, they separate. A simple ceremony conducted by sages in the forest using leaves and flowers is not given much importance, and neither is the thundering of a cloud which is unlikely to result in rain. Similarly, when husband and wife fight "[n]obody takes [them] very seriously. The husband may complain, the wife may complain. Everyone says, 'Yes, yes. That's all right. It will be all right.' They never go to court for divorce."[1]

Historically, some feminists claimed that a woman needs a man like a fish needs a bicycle. Girls are told that they must study and have a career, so that they don't have to depend on a man, and are equipped to walk out of an unpleasant marriage. However, when encouraging women to end their marriage if their spouse is 'pursuing a separate social life' (whatever that means — that he occasionally goes out to dinner with his

1. Lecture by Śrīla Prabhupāda, September 14, 1966.

golfing buddies?), they conveniently forget to mention the consequences. If it's hard for married women to find work-life balance, then it's almost a herculean task for single moms.

An unusually long-term study conducted by economist Kenneth Couch showed that "family structure matters a lot"[1] for women's economic well-being. The study, covering forty years in the lifespan of more than 2,000 women, showed that marriage has such a significant economic benefit for women that even divorcees who develop their own careers successfully cannot match it.

Not only do women have to contend with additional physical and financial strain, but divorce has a far deeper psychological impact on women than society would have us believe. Psychologist Diane Medved, intending to write a book about helping people identify situations in which they should divorce, approached divorced couples expecting to hear that they were over the divorce and had "emerged better for it."[2] She based this on the assumption that people suffering in unhappy marriages ought to get out, and that the jolt of divorce would likely bring about a beneficial psychological change. However, her research forced her to admit that she was wrong: "I had to face the fact that writing a 'morally neutral' book showing divorce to be just another option — a life choice no better or worse than staying married — would be irreparably damaging to the audience I wanted to help."[3]

1. Cindy Weiss, "Divorce is Costly for Women," *UConn Today*, September 28, 2011, archived URL: http://bit.ly/uconcostly

2. Diane Medved, *The Case Against Divorce. Discover the Lures, the Lies, and the Emotional Traps of Divorce-Plus the Seven Vital Reasons to Stay Together* (New York: Ballantine Books, 1990), 3.

3. Ibid., 2.

Instead, Medved compiled *The Case Against Divorce: Discover the Lures, the Lies, and the Emotional Traps of Divorce–Plus the Seven Vital Reasons to Stay Together*, in which she recommends that except for exceptional cases of physical or mental abuse, couples should avoid divorce at all costs, for one cannot undermine how damaging it can be. She emphasizes:

> Divorce was catastrophic — but not in the commonly accepted terms of a single year or two thrown away. I found that the mere contemplation of divorce — the acceptance of it as an imminent option (rather than dedication to working on a wounded marriage) is debilitating. The process of evaluating the injuries — of cajoling and pleading and threatening — is emotionally exhausting. The physical act of packing a bag and moving out is traumatic. And from there the trauma escalates.
>
> Quite simply, I discovered in my research that the process and aftermath of divorce is so pervasively disastrous — to body, mind and spirit — that in an overwhelming number of cases, the "cure" that it brings is surely worse than the marriage's "disease."[1]

Even though divorce is commonplace today, unfortunately, it often lands women in a situation far worse than the one they sought to escape.

Changing Attitudes

In the 1990s, divorce was still unheard of in India. In my large family of aunts and uncles and cousins, we never saw any reconstituted family. Not everyone was happily married, but neither were they bitterly unhappy; either they were happy

1. Ibid., 3–4.

as husband and wife, or reconciled to living with each other's differences. One thing was certain though – as children, we led blissful, carefree lives, for the thought that our parents may separate never crossed our minds. As I grew older, my mother revealed many examples within our extended family of marriages that had hit a rocky patch, but somehow weathered it, and now the couples in question were peacefully living together. There was a distant uncle who was an alcoholic, one who was famous for his bad temper, and another for his whimsical mood swings. There was also an aunt who was very ambitious and constantly nagged and pestered her husband. Yet, the spouses tolerated and stayed with each other, until they mellowed down and eventually gave up their nasty habits. Their children may have seen them bicker and fight, but they also saw that they did not split up, and I expect that must have had a positive effect on them, for in turn each of these children are now happily married.

After I grew up and got married, I looked upon the ladies in my family with new-found admiration. I realized that among adults, specially between husband and wife, there are often disagreements, but in all these years I had never heard my mom or my aunts answer back or snap at either their husbands or anyone older than them, like a mother-in-law or an older sister. This did not mean that they didn't have any say in any matter. On the contrary, we knew that if we wanted to get my father's permission for something, it was best to approach him through my mom, for she always managed to convince him. But I noticed she would not openly oppose his decisions. If she had a difference of opinion, she would usually express it in private. Even if he said something that seemed unfair, she would not kick up a fuss or immediately argue back and forth. When I was younger, I had considered that she was being unnecessarily docile and decided that I would be quite vocal in expressing my views. But practically speaking, I found that actually her strategy worked better. My mother is a lady with strong views of her own, but it was only after I was myself a wife, mother, and daughter-in-law that I could appreciate her expertise at getting her own way each time, without offending anyone, and winning over everyone in the family with her attitude of service and love.

Unfortunately, in India, attitudes regarding marriage and behavior between husband and wife changed significantly, starting with my generation. Perhaps it was the general ethos of championing individuality and not being agreeable or tolerant to one who had a difference of opinion, combined with the influence of cable TV — which arrived in the 90s, with its steamy soap operas like The *Bold and Beautiful,* Oprah Winfrey's talk shows, and movies round the clock — that exposed Indians to an alternate lifestyle. In any case, divorce began to loom as a possible future of a marriage and we started to see marriages end, not just for grievous reasons such as physical abuse, but more often when the couple could not get along. It is, then, no surprise that following the trend, the next generation has an even more casual attitude towards marriage, often choosing to be in live-in relationships instead. While some see this as a sign of progress, particularly for women, alarm bells are ringing for those who are observing the long-term effects of decline of the institution of marriage in Western society.

Saving Grace

My husband and I did not have an arranged marriage. We dated for a considerable period of time before getting married and were confident that our marriage would be smooth sailing, for besides being in love we understood each other well. Yet, to my surprise, it seemed that we were altogether different people when we had to play the role of being husband and wife. The fact that we came from completely different family backgrounds didn't help and the differences in our temperament, which were charming when we were dating, began to grate on our nerves when we were living together 24/7. Since both of us are strong-willed, as is typical of our generation, it is quite likely that, had we allowed ourselves to be dictated by popular sentiment, our ego clashes would have ended in a divorce.

Fortunately, we were both committed to following Vedic injunctions — which ultimately saved our marriage. We learned to put aside our petty differences in favor of maintaining a peaceful atmosphere at home, which is essential if one hopes to make any spiritual advancement. We started to accept our individual roles and gradually grew into them. Just as it was challenging for me to be a submissive wife, it was equally difficult for my husband to understand how to exert his authority without hurting my feelings or coming across as too dictatorial. Ultimately, being convinced that this was a commitment for life helped us to come up with ways and means to move from 'having irreconcilable differences' to 'being happily married.'

I appreciated how he set spiritual goals for our family and he admired how I worked with the children to achieve them. I saw how hard he worked to provide us all the comforts on a single income, and he noted the efforts I put in not only to have a smooth-running house but also to relieve him of

all extra activities like buying groceries, and picking up and dropping the kids, so that he could concentrate on his work. In view of all this, the fact that he is short tempered, or that I'm absent-minded, just didn't seem that important. But we needed the guidance of Vedic culture to endure the initial rocky times and finally come to this stage. We needed the positive role models of our families who are following the traditional culture. And we needed the Vedic vision of having a goal in life that is not just centered on one's personal enjoyment.

Motherhood

In Vedic tradition, women are granted the highest respect because of their role as mothers. The *Vedas* glorify a mother as the epitome of selfless love. Vedic scriptures state that love for God should not be like a business transaction — that we love Him and in return expect Him to fulfill all our demands. Instead, devotion to God means to love and serve Him without expecting anything in return. Śrīla Prabhupāda often explained the concept by comparing it to the unselfish love of a mother for her child.

'Mother' does not mean one who merely performs the biological function of giving birth, but she is an embodiment of sacrifice, nurture, compassion, and comfort. A mother has her child's best interest at heart and is thus the ideal caregiver for the child. To actually care for children is a full-time job, a twenty-four hour responsibility, and a major challenge. And babies require exclusive attention; both parents are permanently on call and may go without proper sleep for days. Although many fathers also take much of the burden, still, the contribution of the mother is irreplaceable — for instance, only she can breastfeed. And actually a woman's innate psychology facilitates her to enjoy being a mother and to sacrifice for her family. Mother's love — in abundance — is essential for raising good children.

Besides taking care of the physical needs of the children, she teaches them to be respectful, truthful, clean, kind and courageous. Therefore, in Vedic civilization the mother is considered to be the first *guru* or honored teacher of the child. As exemplars of selflessness, mothers are vital in contributing to social stability, good population, family values, and religious culture.

A Burden or a Blessing?

Unfortunately, feminists today ridicule the idea of being a full-time mother. Girls are told that they can realize their potential only by having an enlivening career. Children are considered an unnecessary burden; a shackle holding them back in their progressive march towards equality with men. Writer Elske Rahill describes the second-wave feminists' scathing criticism of motherhood.

> The seminal texts from that time — Germaine Greer's famous *The Female Eunuch*, and Betty Friedan's *The Feminine Mystique* — wrote against a world of prescriptive womanhood, where every woman was expected to find full satisfaction in the role of mother and wife. In *The Female Eunuch,* Greer denied the very existence of maternal love, and in *The Feminine*

> *Mystique,* mother-of-three Friedan depicted motherhood as a wasted existence, filled with trivialities, "in lieu of more meaningful goals." Her solution to this meaninglessness was for women to find a fuller identity through commercial work and public participation. The more radical feminist, Shulamith Firestone, saw maternity as the natural reason for women's oppression. "The joy of giving birth," she said, "is a patriarchal myth." She found motherhood deeply unpleasant, and believed that "nothing will change for women as long as natural reproduction remains the rule."[1]

However, being a mother is such a natural thing for a woman (as Rahill discovered to her surprise), that those who do not have children often feel a void in their lives which cannot be filled by professional achievements.

In a particularly heartbreaking article, *My Secret Guilt: Over 35, Single and Childless,* writer Melanie Notkin describes her sorrow at being childless.

> The grief hit me in my mid-thirties without warning.
>
> By all appearances, my life was fantastic, or pretty close. I had a great job in New York City, good friends, some good dates. But then there were times, lonely days and nights, when I would cry. I would sob. I would lie in bed awake for hours, tears running onto my pillow. I was in mourning, but I didn't know it.
>
> Having experienced the same feeling for a few years, I now know the grief was over being childless, or more

1. Elske Rahill, "I loved motherhood. Where does that leave my feminism?" *The Irish Times,* November 8, 2017, archived URL: http://bit.ly/irishmother

> poignantly, over the loss of the baby I never held in my arms. By that point in my life I had expected to be married and a mother to at least two kids. I was far from it, still very single, no kids. Passing by a new mother and her infant strolling down Broadway would rattle my womb. Even seeing a woman swollen from seven or eight months of pregnancy would make my petite frame feel invisible and small. The sadness I'd feel around my period was deeper than hormonal. I was mourning the loss of one more chance at the family life I always dreamed of. [...]
>
> I cautiously hold onto the hope that I may still have a chance to hold my baby in my arms — and that I am still attractive to men who want children too. I know I'm not alone. I am one of the 18 percent of American women between the ages of 40 and 44 who are childless. Pew Research reports that half of this group has chosen that fate; they are childfree by choice. And the rest of us, about one million American childless women ages 40 to 44, suffer from biological or circumstantial infertility.[1]

According to Notkin, many women like her are suffering 'circumstantial infertility' while they are waiting for 'Mr. Right' to show up. Giving priority to studies and their careers, by the time they realize that they want to marry and start a family, there seem to be no eligible bachelors available. Perhaps this is the reason Lori Gottlieb advises young women to settle and marry before it's too late. The staggering statistics quoted by Melanie give an indication why women's infertility has become a cause of concern.

---

1. Melanie Notkin, "My Secret Grief: Over 35, Single and Childless," *HuffPost*, January 18, 2012, archived URL: http://bit.ly/huffpost35

In her article titled *The Sins of Our Feminist Mothers,* and later, in a book called *Wonder Woman; The Myth of Having it All,* ABC TV journalist Virginia Haussegger lashed out at the feminists, when at age 38, she was unable to conceive after being a successful career woman:

> [W]hile encouraging women in the '70s and '80s to reach for the sky, none of our purple clad feminist mothers thought to tell us the truth about the biological clock. Our biological clock. The one that would eventually reach exploding point inside us. [...] But the truth is — for me at least — the career is no longer a challenge, the lifestyle trappings are joyless (the latest Collette Dinnigan frock looks pretty silly on a near-40-year-old), and the point of it all seems, well, pointless. I am childless and I am angry. Angry that I was so foolish to take the word of my feminist mothers as gospel. Angry that I was daft enough to believe female fulfilment came with a leather briefcase. It was wrong. It was crap.[1]

Despite such devastating consequences of their philosophy, feminists refuse to concede that motherhood is an essential part of being a woman and one that is a source of great joy and satisfaction. Sweden is considered to be a feminist paradise. In addition to maternity leave, it allows for fully paid paternity leave. The egalitarian government is urging both mother and father to share the leave equally, and instituted one month as 'daddy leave' which cannot be transferred to the mother. And yet, despite the freedom to split the leave half and half, often mothers take the bulk of the leave, simply because they want to. *The New York Times* reports:

1. Virginia Haussegger, "The Sins of Our Feminist Mothers," *The Age,* July 23, 2002, archived URL: http://bit.ly/FeMomSins

> Swedish mothers still take more time off with children — almost four times as much. And some who thought they wanted their men to help raise baby now find themselves coveting more time at home. [...]
>
> The least enthusiastic [about fathers taking leave to look after the baby], in fact, are often mothers. In a 2003 survey by the Social Insurance Agency, the most commonly cited reason for not taking more paternity leave, after finances, was mother's preference, said Ann-Zofie Duvander, a sociologist at Stockholm University who worked at the agency at the time.
>
> Ann-Marie Prhat of the TCO employee federation said she had been determined to share the parental leave with her husband. After many discussions, "we practically signed a contract — six months for me and six months for him."
>
> Five months into the leave, she was enjoying her son. Could she stay home a couple of months longer, she asked her husband? "In the end," she said, "I negotiated one extra month."[1]

Another woman in liberal Sweden shares her anguish at being forced to join work sooner than she was ready to after having her baby: "It was my maternal instinct to be with my son — every fibre in my being fought against going back [to work]."[2] Pressurized by her employer and relatives, she went back to work after a year, although personally she would have "welcomed the opportunity to stay at home until her son

1. Katrin Benhold, "In Sweden, Men Can Have It All," *The New York Times,* June 9, 2010, archived URL: http://bit.ly/NewYTimes

2. Maddy Savage, "Why Swedish workplaces aren't as equal as you think," *BBC*, May 21, 2017, archived URL: http://bit.ly/BbcSweden

started school." She explains, "There is a societal pressure [...] because everyone goes back to work. I felt I would be going against the norm if I had stayed at home."

Secret Guilt

Relegating motherhood to something mundane and unimportant has led women to either forgo it altogether, or treat it as something part time that can go on side-by-side with their pursuit of a healthy career. Women are told that they should strive to have the right work-life balance (ironically, the very term work-life balance indicates that real life is time spent outside of work) and magically juggle being a career woman, wife, and mother.

Sheryl Sandberg, the current COO of Facebook, in her book *Lean In: Women, Work and the Will to Lead,*[1] urges women to be more aggressive in the workplace and overcome personal inhibitions, such as the desire to be agreeable, that may be keeping them from climbing the corporate ladder. She advises women, "Don't leave before you leave"; in other words, she points out how a pregnant woman backing off from demanding work assignments, or 'leaning back' with the anticipation that she will need more family time soon, is potentially harming her career.

Yet, at the same time, Sandberg herself admitted feeling regret over spending inadequate time with her children:

> I don't have the right answer. I don't even have it for myself. I left San Francisco, where I live, on Monday, and I was

1. Sheryl Sandberg, *Lean In: Women, Work and the Will to Lead* (New York: Alfred A. Knopf, 2013).

> getting on the plane for this conference. And my daughter, who's three, when I dropped her off at preschool, did that whole hugging-the-leg, crying, "Mommy, don't get on the plane" thing. This is hard. I feel guilty sometimes. I know no women, whether they're at home or whether they're in the workforce, who don't feel that sometimes. So I'm not saying that staying in the workforce is the right thing for everyone.[1]

Anne-Marie Slaughter, previously the director of policy planning for the U.S. State Department and the dean of Princeton's Woodrow Wilson School of Public and International Affairs, also writes about struggling to cope with her career and taking care of her teenage sons in her widely read article *Why Women Still Can't Have It All* (2012). She explains the reason for quitting her high-profile job in Washington:

> I realized that I didn't just *need* to go home. Deep down, I *wanted* to go home. I wanted to be able to spend time with my children in the last few years that they are likely to live at home, crucial years for their development into responsible, productive, happy, and caring adults.[2]

She emphasizes that it's particularly difficult for a woman to handle being away from the children.

> Still, the proposition that women can have high-powered careers as long as their husbands or partners are willing to share the parenting load equally (or disproportionately)

---

1. Sheryl Sandberg, "Why we have too few women leaders," *TED,* December 2010, archived URL: http://bit.ly/TedSheryl

2. Anne-Marie Slaughter, "Why Women Still Can't Have It All," *The Atlantic,* July-August, 2012, archived URL: http://bit.ly/atlanticant

> assumes that most women will *feel* as comfortable as men do about being away from their children, as long as their partner is home with them. In my experience, that is simply not the case.
>
> Here I step onto treacherous ground, mined with stereotypes. From years of conversations and observations, however, I've come to believe that men and women respond quite differently when problems at home force them to recognize that their absence is hurting a child, or at least that their presence would likely help. I do not believe fathers love their children any less than mothers do, but men do seem more likely to choose their job at a cost to their family, while women seem more likely to choose their family at a cost to their job.
>
> Many factors determine this choice, of course. Men are still socialized to believe that their primary family obligation is to be the breadwinner; women, to believe that their primary family obligation is to be the caregiver. But it may be more than that. When I described the choice between my children and my job to Senator Jeanne Shaheen, she said exactly what I felt: "There's really no choice." She wasn't referring to social expectations, but to a maternal imperative felt so deeply that the "choice" is reflexive.

Slaughter points out that Mary Matalin, President Bush's assistant and Vice President Cheney's counselor, felt the same way. Matalin quit her job when she realized that it was possible for someone else to take over her professional responsibilities but no one could replace her as the mother of her children: "I'm indispensable to my kids, but I'm not close to indispensable to the White House."

Slaughter muses that there is no perfect way of planning one's career such that one can be there when the kids need it: "[I] f you have children earlier, you may have difficulty getting a graduate degree, a good first job, and opportunities for advancement in the crucial early years of your career. Making matters worse, you will also have less income while raising your children, and hence less ability to hire the help that can be indispensable to your juggling act." On the other hand, establishing one's career first and having children in mid to late 30s "raises the possibility of spending long, stressful years and a small fortune trying to have a baby" and "it means that many peak career opportunities are coinciding precisely with their teenage years, when, experienced parents advise, being available as a parent is just as important as in the first years of a child's life."

It seems PepsiCo's CEO, Indra K. Nooyi largely agrees with Slaughter. She told David Bradley, owner of *The Atlantic* magazine, that despite having both family members and hired help at home to assist in bringing up her two daughters, she wasn't sure whether her daughters would say that she's been a good mom. Missing important events in her children's life made her feel very guilty. Nooyi confides:

> You know, you have to cope, because you die with guilt. You just die with guilt. My observation, David, is that the biological clock and the career clock are in total conflict with each other. Total, complete conflict. When you have to have kids you have to build your career. Just as you're rising to middle management your kids need you because they're teenagers, they need you for the teenage years.[1]

---

1. Conor Friedersdorf, "Why PepsiCo CEO Indra K. Nooyi Can't Have It All," *The Atlantic*, July 1, 2014, archived URL: http://bit.ly/atlanticpepsi

And yet, none of these successful women can imagine being full-time moms for their entire lives, nor do they give such advice to younger women who look up to them as role models. According to them, the solution is that the corporates need to be more accommodating, and fathers need to pitch in and do their bit. And, in the interim period, while waiting for these measures to be put in place, Sandberg advises the women to 'lean in,' ask for the raise they deserve and push their way to the top. Nooyi suggests setting up a strong support system by roping in family members, hiring nannies, and training secretaries to answer the children's calls if the mother is busy in a meeting.

However, for the majority of working women, secretaries or full-time nannies are a luxury they cannot afford. Most have to settle for day care centers which are either expensive or poorly run. Describing the abysmal condition of some of the day care centers, Jonathan Cohn observes:

> This situation is especially disturbing because, over the past two decades, researchers have developed an entirely new understanding of the first few years of life. This period affects the architecture of a child's brain in ways that indelibly shape intellectual abilities and behavior. Kids who grow up in nurturing, interactive environments tend to develop the skills they need to thrive as adults — like learning how to calm down after a setback or how to focus on a problem long enough to solve it. Kids who grow up without that kind of attention tend to lack impulse control and have more emotional outbursts. Later on, they are more likely to struggle in school or with the law. They also have more physical health problems. Numerous studies

> show that all children, especially those from low-income homes, benefit greatly from sound child care.[1]

Cohn's solution is for the American government to support the working women by developing the infrastructure for state-funded or subsidized day care centers, for "[w]hen parents can find safe, affordable child care, they are more likely to realize their full economic potential. Their employers gain, too." According to economists quoted by Cohn, "the most efficient means to boost the productivity of the workforce 15 to 20 years down the road is to invest in today's youngest children" and that such spending would yield "a much higher return than most government-funded economic development initiatives." It seems like it would be a win-win situation — the parents earn more, their employers are happy and the children grow up to be efficient little cogs in the future economic framework.

However, even if one were to accept Cohn's idea of assessing individuals on the merit of their economic worth, not everyone agrees with him that "investing in today's youngest children" is equivalent to building a better day center infrastructure. Journalist Jonas Himmelstrand, who recently investigated the public day care system in Sweden, which is touted internationally as ideal because of its high standards and affordability, cautions: "Before other countries copy Sweden's public daycare system, they should be careful to consider what the results have been."[2] He states that "rapidly

---

1. Jonathan Cohn, "The Hell of American Day Care," *The New Republic*, April 15, 2013, archived URL: http://bit.ly/HellDayCare

2. Jonas Himmelstrand, "Swedish Daycare: International Example or Cautionary Tale," *IMFC, Institute of Marriage and Family Canada*, September 10, 2015, archived URL: http://bit.ly/imfcanaday

declining psychological health of the youth," "plummeting school results" and "disorder in the Swedish classrooms," may have some correlation to the fact that "[o]ver 90 percent of all 18 month to 5-years-olds are in daycare."

One of the arguments offered in support of outsourcing child care is that the children will be looked after by trained individuals. Actually, there is some truth in this for these days young parents are unprepared or insecure about shouldering the responsibility of being their children's primary caregivers. Women are taught math, science and geography but have little idea about the needs of an infant. Nevertheless, as evidenced by the Swedish day care system, the exclusive care and attention that a child receives from his mother cannot be compared to that given by a trained, but indifferent, professional.

In traditional societies, children are cherished and the family structure allows them to remain in close proximity of several loving family members. The mother remains with the child almost exclusively till he is two years old — it's a common sight to see a mother going about her chores with her baby on her hip — and at the same time, there are grandparents, aunts, uncles and older siblings to look over him. The girls learn to take care of younger children very early on and receive hands-on training for motherhood as they are growing up. Also, by being in the company of their own mothers, they observe and learn techniques of parenting such as striking the balance between being indulgent and strict, giving encouragement and constructive criticism, and keeping the children productively engaged. These days, scores of books and websites are dedicated to listing useful parenting tips that previously people picked up simply by being raised in a healthy family environment.

In Vedic culture, the idea of "investing" in the children was to give them ample love and affection and to teach them to adhere to high moral standards. The onus was, to a large extent, on the mother, particularly when the children were younger.

Game Changer

All the mothers that I've spoken with agree that giving birth was a life-altering experience for them. I concur. I was unprepared for the overwhelming rush of affection that I felt when I held my babies. I was surprised at how ungrudgingly I looked after their every need and how excruciatingly I felt their pain when they were hurt. It was strange for an inherently selfish person like me to look up recipes on the Internet, and experiment with cooking and baking, just to hear their squeals of joy and watch them gleefully devour the treats. I began to understand what it means to love someone selflessly.

Stranger still was that my fondness wasn't for my daughters alone. Suddenly I began to notice and pay attention to children wherever I went — I would tear up looking at the state of the poor children who line the streets of Delhi, I would be sympathetic instead of irritated at the cries of an infant in an airplane squirming in his seat belt during take-off, and I would find myself wanting to comfort and rock whichever baby was crying.

Naturally, we wanted the best for our daughters. From Vedic scriptures, we learnt that parenting wasn't simply a matter of feeding and clothing the children, taking them for art classes, or keeping money aside for their college education. We understood that besides looking after our girls' physical and emotional needs, the most important part of parenting was to help our children in their spiritual journey. Accordingly, right from the beginning, we spent a lot of time explaining Vedic philosophy to them, and also engaging them in practical devotional service such as decorating the altar with fresh flowers, cleaning the paraphernalia required for worship, and helping to cook the offering. Being parents inspires us to be better devotees ourselves, for Śrīla Prabhupāda emphasizes that the most effective way to teach is to show by example.

I find my role as a mother of the two lovely little individuals entrusted to my care to be brilliantly fulfilling, and wonder why anyone would find it belittling to be addressed as mother of so-and-so, rather than, say, managing director of such-and-such company.

Just as Lori Gottlieb advises young women to settle down and marry without delay, my advice is that once married, one should go ahead and have children sooner, rather than later and preferably more than one. After I gave birth to my daughter within a year of being married, my sister and sister-in-law, who are both older than me (and had married before me, but had delayed having children to concentrate on their careers), were inspired to have children of their own. They, then, promptly had two children each, in quick succession, for they were so happy with their experience of motherhood. My sister admitted that she felt foolish for having put off something so special for so long.

The other day I saw a little girl, no older than two or three years old, cradling a baby doll in her arms. As I watched her carrying the doll everywhere with her, hugging her, setting her down carefully, sometimes mock-scolding her and sometimes feeding her make-believe food with a toy spoon, I marveled at how deep the maternal instinct is. Surely her mom would not have spent hours teaching the little girl, who was hardly more than a baby herself, how to take care of a doll, yet here she was — a perfect little mom to her tiny little doll.

It is sad that today our lives are fashioned in such a way that this natural desire to be a mother has to be suppressed and postponed, sometimes almost indefinitely. Once, when my daughter was six months old, I went to see a doctor, accompanied by my best friend from college. Later, my friend confided in me that when I had mentioned to the doctor that I was a nursing mother, she had felt an intense longing to be a mother herself. But she and her husband had decided that it wasn't the right time for them, for they wanted to study further and work on their careers first. Over the next several years we discussed this topic often, but each time it seemed that there was something preventing them from taking the plunge — at first it was her post-graduate course, later her doctorate program, and then waiting to get secure jobs. Eventually, she did give birth to a lovely little girl — although almost eight years after we had that initial conversation. Fortunately for her, things worked out as she had planned, but there are others, like Virginia Haussegger, who have to live with the regret of having left it until it was too late.

Giving birth is a magical experience, it's an exceptional privilege granted to women — no woman should be deprived of it.

Education and Career

In the Vedic system, education was more practical than the current system of 'one size fits all.' This means that children were trained according to their propensities. They did not spend most of their childhood learning a mix of language, math, science, and humanities, only to specialize much later. In fact, many children did not go to school.

Education means to impart knowledge, values, and skills. According to the Vedic understanding, knowledge is that which is contained in the *Vedas*, the essence of which is to establish our relationship with God. Schools or *gurukulas* were meant to impart this knowledge, and only children who had the inclination to study subjects contained in the *Vedas* such as philosophy, medicine and astronomy would undergo formal education. Those who did not have the caliber to delve deep into the *Vedas* would receive this knowledge in the form of simple stories by the elders in the family. At the same time, by working alongside their fathers from a young age, they would learn skills which would help them earn their livelihood. The farmer would train his children at home, as would the trader, the craftsman, the barber, and so on.

Apart from knowledge and skills, one of the most important aspects of Vedic education was to teach values to the children. Character building was considered to be more important than acquiring skills to get a job. The boys in the *gurukula* were trained as *brahmacārīs*, or celibate monks. They were taught self-control and to look upon every woman, except their future wife, as their mother.

Girls did not go to school, but they too received knowledge, values and skills. They were home-schooled, as were several boys. Regarding acquiring knowledge of the *Vedas*, if they belonged to a family of *brāhmaṇas*, the priests and teachers of the *Vedas*, they might receive instruction from their fathers, and after they were married, from their husbands. The girls in the *kṣatriya* families, the royal family and their ministers, would sometimes have formal tutors. Otherwise, most girls received Vedic knowledge in a simplified way from their mother and grandmother, who would narrate stories from the scriptures, particularly *Rāmāyaṇa* and *Mahābhārata*. There are examples in the scriptures of qualified women well-versed in philosophy, for example, as evidenced in the wonderful prayers of Queen Kuntī.[1]

Śrīmad-Bhāgavatam describes the incident when Satī, the wife of Lord Śiva, infuriated and embarrassed by her father, Dakṣa, and

1. *Śrīmad-Bhāgavatam* 1.8.18–43.

his offensive behavior towards her husband, decided to sever her relationship with him by giving up her present body and transferring herself to a new body, that of the daughter of the king of mountains. In his purport, Śrīla Prabhupāda describes how "Satī sat down on the ground and faced north. Dressed in saffron garments, she sanctified herself with water and closed her eyes to absorb herself in the process of mystic yoga."[1] Finally she "quit her body in a blazing fire by meditation on the fiery elements."[2] In this context, Śrīla Prabhupāda comments:

> Satī was the wife of Lord Śiva, who is known as Yogeśvara, the best among all *yogīs,* because he knows all the mystic processes of *yoga,* so it appeared that Satī also knew them. Either she learned *yoga* from her husband or she was enlightened because she was the daughter of such a great king as Dakṣa.[3]

The most important thing that the girls learnt as part of their education, however, was how to conduct themselves in a respectable manner. Just as the boys were trained in the principle of *bramacarya* in the *gurukula*, the girls were trained in chastity. Such values were conveyed to the children through direct instruction, as well as through the example of the grown-ups around them who practiced these principles.

In addition, in the company of the women and older girls, the girls learnt skills that would help them to take care of their families in future. They developed expertise in treating common illnesses through natural home remedies, utilizing herbs and spices to prepare brews that could cure fevers, colds,

1. *Śrīmad-Bhāgavatam* 4.4.24.
2. *Śrīmad-Bhāgavatam* 4.4.27.
3. *Śrīmad-Bhāgavatam* 4.4.24, purport by Śrīla Prabhupāda.

upset stomachs, headaches and fatigue. They learnt how to keep the house in order and how to manage the household expenses, how to welcome guests, look after the elderly, entertain the younger children, how to paint, and how to sew, knit, embroider and darn.

The young ladies learnt to cook, and were trained not just in preparing the main course, but also in preparing all kinds of sweets and snacks, and pickles and preserves. It was believed that any food cooked was infused with the consciousness of the chef, so even a simple dish prepared lovingly at home was considered far healthier than something fancy picked up from a restaurant.

Cooking is particularly significant in the Vedic tradition. Everything prepared at home was first offered on the altar to the deities before being served to the rest of the family. In that sense, it was an act of worship, and the kitchen itself was considered to be an extension of the altar and maintained with strict standards of cleanliness. The Vedic culture emphasizes that God is a person and every individual can have a unique relationship with Him. The ladies understood that their deity at home is God Himself, appearing out of His sweet will to accept their devotion and bless them. Thus cooking was not just a mundane chore but yet another opportunity to meditate on the Lord and attempt to please Him. Similarly, cleaning the house was equivalent to cleaning a temple, and taking care of the children was important so that they would grow up to be good devotees of the Lord; every aspect of their day-to-day life was significant for it was connected to the Supreme Lord of the universe.

Women were happy to be engaged in the work at home, seeing it as service to the Lord, and understanding that if it is performed with a humble attitude and the right consciousness, it is as pleasing to the Lord as the formal worship offered by the priests in the temple. Lord Krsna is known as *bhāva-grāhī* — one who accepts the spirit of devotion. *Śrīmad-Bhāgavatam* mentions that when Lord Kṛṣṇa was departing from Hastināpura, the ladies began discussing His pastimes and glorifying Him in their simple language. This pleased Him more than the choicest mantras in the scriptures: "Absorbed in the thought of the transcendental qualities of the Lord, who is sung in select poetry, the ladies on the roofs of all the houses of Hastināpura began to talk of Him. This talk was more attractive than the hymns of the *Vedas*."[1]

Apart from such generic skills, the girls were trained to develop expertise in particular subject matters, depending on the families into which they were born, and into which they were likely to be married. For example, girls in a family of *brāhmaṇas* would learn Sanskrit mantras and methods of worship in order to be able to assist their husbands. Similarly, *kṣatriya* girls may learn horse-riding. The *Rāmāyaṇa* describes that when King Daśaratha was wounded in battle, his wife, Kaikeyī, guided their chariot to a safe place and nursed him back to health. It seems *kṣatriya* girls were also trained in diplomacy, for scriptures often describe how the wives would advise their husbands in political affairs. In the *Rāmāyaṇa*, when King Vāli's brother Sugrīva challenged him to a duel, his wife Tārā advised him against it, for on previous occasions Sugrīva had been badly defeated by Vāli, and she presumed that his

1. *Śrīmad-Bhāgavatam* 1.10.20.

new-found confidence indicated that he had formed an alliance with a powerful personality. Vāli disregarded her advice and met his death, for it was indeed as she had suspected — Sugrīva had allied with the undefeatable Lord Rāma.

So the girls too would receive what may be considered vocational training, but it was with the view of allowing them to be helpful to their husbands and continuing the family tradition by teaching the children. They were not expected to go and earn their own living based on their education. For them to do so would be considered a failure on the part of their family to provide for them and keep them satisfied. Even in situations where the family was so poor that the women also had to contribute to the household income, it would be managed in such a way that they could do it while remaining at home. For example, they would weave baskets, make handicrafts, or prepare sweets and savories, which their husband would sell either door to door or at the marketplace.

In Vedic culture, a woman's 'career' was to look after the household affairs and that was a full-time job that kept her busy throughout the day. In fact, the women often worked harder than the men: "a man's work is from sun to sun but a woman's work is never done." And yet, they were peaceful for they were surrounded by loving family members. They could work on their own terms and had the flexibility to rest when they were feeling tired. They had the satisfaction of managing the household efficiently and watching their children blossom under their watchful eyes. And along with their day to day work, they were able to indulge their creative sides by pursuing projects such as painting pictures, embroidering elaborate bedspreads or crocheting sweaters.

These ladies did not feel that there was something missing in their lives, or that they had to work in a large organization or research lab to rise to their potential. Moreover, they had no desire to strive hard for a second income at the risk of jeopardizing their household harmony, for Vedic culture teaches the ideal of simple living. As seen in princess Devahūti's case, even royal princesses would adjust to an austere lifestyle, if that's what the husband was able to offer them. The ladies knew how to make ends meet with whatever income the husband brought home. Also, it was not the case that since the man alone was earning, his wife would have no claims to the money. The man's earnings were considered to be the family income and the wife would have the freedom to use it at her discretion, albeit with the husband's consent for major decisions.

Furthermore, the housewives of Vedic times did not have to wonder how they would occupy themselves once the kids had flown the coop. They welcomed the opportunity to delve deeper into their spiritual lives by traveling with their husbands to places of pilgrimage, attending discourses by saintly people, performing more service at the temple, reading the scriptures and absorbing themselves in meditation. At the same time, they played an important role as advisors to the younger ladies in the family. Their daughters, daughters-in-law, grandchildren and even great-grandchildren looked up to them for guidance.

Deprecating the Housewives

The model of men going out to work and the ladies staying to manage the home front — currently dubbed 'traditional gender roles' — has existed universally, all over the world, for many centuries. In Sanskrit, a wife is called *gṛha-lakṣmī,* 'the goddess of fortune within the home,' or *gṛhiṇī* (commonly rendered in Hindi as *gharwālī*), 'the lady at home.' In English, this model is summarized by the (now almost defunct) saying: "A woman's place is in the home."

However, today the word 'housewife' is almost a derogatory word, for it is understood that if you don't have a job outside the house, you are either just stupid or a repressed victim of the patriarchy. The modern woman seeks fulfillment through a career. Her very desire to do so is complexly linked with the historical transformation of the economy from an agrarian to an industrial one, and the almost complete shift in values, norms, and behaviors that accompanied the age of technology. One effect was that women's work, which had been performed in the home, lost its economic value because much of the housework that they used to do could now be done by machines. Additionally, by utilizing artificial contraception, they were now bearing fewer children.

As per Betty Friedan, author of the highly influential *The Feminine Mystique*, the storybook-perfect housewives of her time (the 1960s) were "bored and listless" and "nervous and jittery."[1] Of the women whom she interviewed, a surprising number were regularly treated by psychotherapists or often took tranquilizers; and several had attempted suicide. Many also were engaged — "in fact or in fantasy" — in extramarital affairs.[2] To Friedan, their plight was obvious: "[T]hey had uncommon gifts of intelligence and ability nourished by at least the beginnings of higher education — and the life they were leading as suburban housewives denied them the full

1. Betty Friedan, *The Feminine Mystique*, 1963 (London: Penguin Classics, 2010), 192.

2. Ibid., 191.

use of their gifts."[1] Friedan reasoned that if women do not use their natural gifts in livelihoods commensurate with their abilities, the idleness of their domestic home life will be the cause of their perpetual misery.

However, Friedan's proposed solution was not without its own set of problems. For one thing, later and more rigorous studies have shown that the extramarital affairs that Friedan presumed were caused by household boredom did not cease when women found their way into the workforce. Instead, the workplace offered further opportunity for illicit affairs. As reported by a recent study: "Some researchers have found that around one-half of participants who had cheated on their partner and who sought therapy (due to problems in their primary relationship) had met their extradyadic partner [paramour] through their work."[2]

Going to work seemed to be an exciting alternative to women who were bored at home. And yet, most jobs have a wearying monotony that does nothing to alleviate the listlessness that the women may have faced at home. According to the business journal *Gallup,* only 13% of employees worldwide are "involved in, enthusiastic about and committed to their work and workplace."[3] No doubt the women are now able to apply their "uncommon gifts of intelligence and ability" in

1. Ibid., 192.

2. Kristen P. Mark, Erick Janssen and Robin Milhausen, "Infidelity in Heterosexual Couples: Demographic, Interpersonal, and Personality-Related Predictors of Extradyadic Sex," *Archives of Sexual Behavior* 40, no. 5 (2011) 971–82. doi: 10.1007/s10508-011-9771-z.

3. Annamarie Mann and Jim Harter, "The Worldwide Employee Engagement Crisis," *Gallup*, January 7, 2016, archived URL: http://bit.ly/gallupcrisis

increasing profits of the corporates for whom they work, but this happens often at the cost of their own peace of mind. Unfortunately, as evidenced by the *Gallup* statistics, at the end of the day, jobs are not accompanied with the sense of fulfillment that they seem to promise.

Traditional Gender Roles: Oppression or Social Well-Being?

Women's activists have generally advocated that traditional gender roles were devised by men to 'keep the women in their place,' relegating them to remain in the background while their husbands and fathers go out to slay the dragons and achieve all the glory and adoration. Activists figured that the women too should be given an equal opportunity to be dragon-slayers and thus began an entire movement dedicated to teaching women to be as aggressive and competitive as men. Indeed, now women can be anything from fire fighters to army commandos and such achievers are held up as role models for little girls.

Disney has released movies such as *Brave,* in which the lead character Merida is an expert horse-rider and archer who effortlessly defeats all the princes who have come to compete for her hand in marriage. *Mulan* is about a Chinese girl who disguises herself as a boy, joins the army, and goes on to become a hero when she rescues the Emperor from an assault by the Huns. *Moana* depicts the story of a young girl who sails across the ocean alone, battling demons and pirates to restore balance to her world. Movies such as *Kill Bill, Lara Croft: Tomb Raider, GI Jane,* and *Wonder Woman* further glamorize the idea that women can be as good as men in everything, including being trained fighters capable of violently killing anyone who comes in their way.

However, at a time when 'equal opportunity' has successfully been delivered to women around the world, particularly in developed countries, they are beginning to question whether 'manning up' is what they truly want. Although women's groups have struggled for decades to break traditional gender roles with the firm belief that they are detrimental to a woman's real interest, when given a choice, many independent-minded women, of their own accord, are opting to embrace them.

Author of *The War Against Boys* and *Freedom Feminism: Its Surprising History — and Why it Matters,* Christina Hoff Sommers questions Sheryl Sandberg's presentation of an ideal society. In her book *Lean In: Women, Work, and the Will to Lead,* Sandberg states that a true equality would be achieved when 50% of top leadership positions are assigned to women, and 50% of households are managed by men. Hoff Sommers wonders whether breaking free of gender stereotypes is "truly liberating."[1] She points out that research conducted across fifty-five nations indicates that the more economically prosperous and educated a society is and the more freedom the people are given to choose their roles, the more they tend to move towards traditional roles: "Women tend to be more nurturing, risk averse and emotionally expressive, while men are usually more competitive, risk taking, and emotionally flat."

Hoff Sommers refutes Sandberg's claim that Western women are not adequately represented in STEM (science, technology,

1. Christina Hoff Sommers, "What 'Lean In' Misunderstands About Gender Differences," *The Atlantic,* May 19, 2013, archived URL: http://bit.ly/atlanticgendiff

engineering and mathematics) fields due to discrimination, instead suggesting that American women "have more opportunities to pursue careers that really interest them," so they make a deliberate choice not to study subjects such as engineering.

In her article *The More Gender Equality, the Fewer Women in STEM,*[1] journalist Olga Khazan explores the paradox that in countries that empower women, women are less likely to choose math and science professions. It appears that in wealthier countries, where women are not constrained by the financial lucrativeness of a profession, and they are given an opportunity to pick one that truly interests them, they tend to gravitate towards those which are more 'feminine' in nature.

In addition, Hoff Sommers quotes survey results from Pew research Center, which appear to indicate that mothers would much rather be working part-time or not at all, compared to fathers who by and large prefer to work full time. In fact, the higher the socio-economic status, the less likely women are to choose full-time work. Hoff Sommers comments: "Sandberg regards such attitudes as evidence of women's fear of success, double standards, gender bias, sexual harassment, and glass ceilings. But what if they are the triumph of prosperity and opportunity?"[2]

Continuing in the same vein, Margaret Wente, one of Canada's leading columnists, writes:

---

1. Olga Khazan, "The More Gender Equality, the Fewer Women in STEM," *The Atlantic,* Feb 18, 2018, archived URL: http://bit.ly/STEMUnequal
2. Hoff Sommers, "What 'Lean In' Misunderstands."

> Sweden and the other Nordic nations always seem to lead the rankings of the world's best countries for women. (Canada is lucky to crack the top 20.) So they're an ideal laboratory for finding out what women really want. What choices will women make when the playing field is as level as social policy can make it?
>
> I'm afraid the answers will disappoint a lot of people. That includes Sheryl Sandberg, the famous author of *Lean In*, who wrote, "A truly equal world would be one where women ran half our countries and companies, and men ran half our homes."
>
> The trouble is that the world's most liberated women aren't leaning in — in fact, many are leaning back. They work fewer hours and make less money than men, just as Canadian women do. In fact, Swedish women are much more likely to have part-time jobs and far less likely to hold top managerial positions or be CEOs. On top of that, Scandinavian labour markets are the most gender-segregated in the developed world.[1]

Thus in advanced countries women are choosing not to work at all, or to work part-time, and even in their choice of careers tend to opt for those which are more suited to their inherent nature of nurturing and caring. Hoff Sommers, therefore, asks the pertinent question: "What if gender difference turns out to be a phenomenon not of oppression, but rather of social well-being?"[2]

---

1. Margaret Wente, "Do women really have it better in Sweden?" *The Globe and Mail,* 2018, January 23, archived URL: http://bit.ly/swedenwomen
2. Hoff Sommers, "What 'Lean In' Misunderstands."

This, in fact, is the Vedic understanding. Each individual has his or her inherent nature and is most satisfied when they are engaged accordingly. Women's needs are best served when they are protected and provided for and given the chance to be peacefully at home. In Vedic times, women would utilize their natural "gifts of intelligence and ability" (Friedan, 1963) in maintaining beautiful houses, preparing innovative culinary delights, creating works of art and poetry, raising responsible children, and running their household with the efficiency of a military establishment. These ladies were not idle or lazy, nor were they frustrated due to lack of accomplishment. They had the time of the day to think about God and teach their children to bow down before Him. They commanded respect, not because of the salary they brought home but because of their gentle and loving nature and their quiet dedication towards serving their family. Such ladies may not have received any 'Employee of the year awards,' and yet at the end of the day, they felt that their cup was full.

For instance, an entire section of the ancient epic *Mahābhārata* is devoted to the joys and responsibilities of housewifery. It is recorded as a conversation between Lord Kṛṣṇa's wife Satyabhāmā and Draupadī, in which Satyabhāmā marvels at the marital harmony of Draupadī and her husbands, the Pāṇḍavas. Draupadī explains that she is happy to be engaged throughout the day in personally serving her husbands and managing other aspects of their household, which includes keeping track of the expenses, ensuring that the *brāhmaṇas* and other guests are appropriately honored, and handling maid servants, cowherds, shepherds and other attendants. Draupadī's devotion and diligence had won her husbands over to the point that there was no discord among them.

In the present day, countries proudly announce that women will also be fighting on the front lines of battle, citing it as a shining example of offering equal opportunity to women to pursue whichever path they want. But according to Vedic culture it would be considered a matter of national shame if women are placed in a situation where they run a real risk of being killed, tortured or sexually harassed.

One may argue that some, if not the majority of women, have the physical and mental capability to be in active combat, and if such women choose to serve their country in this way, why should there be an objection? Similarly, there are women who are expert and capable as managers and heads of companies; women whose inclusion in corporations and board rooms brings to the table a more diverse outlook towards things which ultimately helps to bring in more profits. There are women who would rather be standing up and giving a presentation to a room full of people about economic trends in the coming year, than humming in the kitchen, baking cookies. Why hold these ladies back in their personal quest for happiness by imposing old-fashioned gender roles?

The answer lies in examining the long term impact of these changes. Capt. Katie Petronio, a combat engineer officer with 5 years of active service and two combat deployments, one to Iraq and the other to Afghanistan, writes:

> In the end, my main concern is not whether women are capable of conducting combat operations, as we have already proven that we can hold our own in some very difficult combat situations; instead, my main concern is a question of longevity. Can women endure the physical and

> physiological rigors of sustained combat operations, and are we willing to accept the attrition and medical issues that go along with integration?

Speaking from her own experience, she says,

> Five years later, I am physically not the woman I once was and my views have greatly changed on the possibility of women having successful long careers while serving in the infantry. I can say from firsthand experience in Iraq and Afghanistan, and not just emotion, that we haven't even begun to analyze and comprehend the gender-specific medical issues and overall physical toll continuous combat operations will have on females.[1]

Similarly, in other areas of work that are physically less intensive, while it may be initially gratifying, eventually when the desire to have a family becomes too strong to ignore, the physical stress of maintaining the perfect balance between work and home often becomes overwhelming. Many women who put off getting married and having children until much later for the sake of their careers are now part of what is being dubbed as the sandwich generation, due to their being 'sandwiched' between taking care of young children and ailing parents at the same time.

Part of the answer also lies in analyzing the impact of an individual's decision on the larger society, and in examining the trends that are set for future generations. Even if it is rewarding for some women to pursue a career (and they have somehow worked out the perfect work-life balance for the time

---

1. Capt. Katie Petronio, "Get Over It! We Are Not All Created Equal," *Marine Corps Gazette* 97, no. 3 (March, 2013).

being), and it is economically beneficial for the organizations they work for, if these women emerge as the only possible role models, this immediately denigrates the thousands of other women who would otherwise have been perfectly happy to be housewives. While it would be considered preposterous in this day and age to suggest that no women should have a career outside of their home, if career women are inordinately glorified over all those who are contributing in other ways, it discourages the homemakers and creates a situation in society where home is no longer the peaceful haven it used to be, for housework and child care are viewed as mind-numbing work which requires no talent. That which ought to have been an exception has today become the general rule, and women who would have ordinarily been happy enough to be homebodies find themselves bowing to societal expectations and getting caught in a chaos of careers.

Although women activists champion the idea that a woman should be free to decide who she wants to be, the unspoken part of the refrain is 'so long as she doesn't decide to be a worthless housewife.' Ann Oakley, the British feminist, wrote: "Housework is work directly opposed to the possibility of human self-actualisation."[1] Simone De Beauvoir paints a similarly depressing picture about the fate of the housewife:

> Few tasks are more like the torture of Sisyphus than housework, with its endless repetition: the clean becomes soiled, the soiled is made clean, over and over, day after day. The housewife wears herself out marking time: she makes nothing, simply perpetuates the present [...] Eating, sleeping, cleaning — the years no longer rise up towards

1. Ann Oakley, *Housewife* (London: Penguin, 1974), 222.

> heaven, they lie spread out ahead, grey and identical. The battle against dust and dirt is never won.[1]

In a similar vein, Betty Friedan writes that housewives suffered a slow death of mind and spirit: "[T]he women who 'adjust' as housewives, who grow up wanting to be 'just a housewife,' are in as much danger as the millions who walked to their own death in the concentration camps [...]."[2]

The feminists proclaimed that it's better to be a prostitute who is paid for her 'services,' than to be a housewife who toils without getting any tangible income in return. Such derisive contempt for work related to the home on the one hand, and admiration for any work outside of it on the other, sets women up for a conflicted existence. The desire to work towards having a clean, attractive house, well-groomed and well-behaved children, and a relationship of servitude towards their spouse must now be suppressed and disregarded as insignificant compared to the importance of achieving accolades in their work life. Not only that, when feminists criticize the role of a homemaker, they are criticizing more than 50% of women all over the world.[3] Oakley and Friedan's intentions may have been to liberate them from the perceived grind of boring housework, but in the process, they have performed a great disservice to a large number of women by robbing them of the dignity of their natural roles as housewives.

A significant difference in attitudes is reflected here. Modern secular society gives considerable prominence to material

1. Simone de Beauvoir, *The Second Sex,* 1949, trans. Constance Borde and Sheila Malovany-Chevallier (New York: Vintage Books, 2011), 487.
2. Friedan, *The Feminine Mystique,* 247.
3. "The World's Women 2015, Chapter 4: Work," *United Nations,* assessed 15 July, 2018, archived URL: http://bit.ly/unstatgen

achievements, measured in terms of wealth and position. In Vedic culture, however, acquiring knowledge and building character were considered the highest goals of life. The class of people most respected were those who were well-versed in the Vedic scriptures, who acted as priests and teachers, and who lived in very humble conditions. Even great kings bowed down before them; it did not matter that they were not making a tangible economic contribution to society. Similarly, a respectable housewife diligently following her duties at home was considered as important to the family and society as the men who were going out and earning the daily bread.

Return of the Housewife

It appears as if things are coming full circle, for despite all the propaganda against it, a small but growing minority of young women are choosing to stay home full time, like their great-grandmothers. Ada Slivinski writes in her article, *The Return of the Housewife:*

> It seems that as life gets busier, we as a society are starting to place more value on the domestic arts. It's a great thing. Homemaker blogs and social media accounts like Naomi Davis' *Love Taza* are attracting massive followings. It's part of return to appreciating the simple things — family, food and a beautiful home. [...] According to a study conducted by the Pew Research Center in 2014, the percentage of women who do not work outside the home is rising. In 1999, 23 percent of all mothers stayed at home while in 2012, 29 percent did.[1]

---

1. Ada Slivinski, "The Return of the Housewife," *Mercatonet*, February 15, 2016, archived URL: http://bit.ly/HWifeReturns

Author of *Expecting: The Inner Life of Pregnancy,* Chitra Ramaswamy describes her unexpectedly positive experience of being a housewife in an article she wrote for *The Guardian.* When she realized that she could not afford quality childcare for her son, she decided to be a housewife, hoping that "no matter how dull, frustrating, and lonely life might get,"[1] she wouldn't regret it. However, she was pleasantly surprised:

> What I didn't expect was to love it so much. To get satisfaction from a job that impresses no one despite incorporating every skill known to humanity. You may wonder what's to love about work that gives me two hours off a day (until the night shift begins), yet the 2014 UK national well-being index revealed that mothers who stay at home have a stronger sense that their lives are "worthwhile" than the rest of society.

Ramaswamy is one of the women who claim that being a feminist and a housewife do not have to be mutually exclusive. If feminism truly supports a woman's right to make her own choices, being a homemaker should be encouraged and celebrated as much as being a career woman.

In her article *When I Became A Mother, Feminism Let Me Down,* Samantha Johnson explores some of the damaging effects of living in a society that "pretends the women don't grow up to be mothers."[2]

---

1. Chitra Ramaswamy, "I love being a housewife and that doesn't make me any less of a feminist," *The Guardian,* March 2, 2015, archived URL: http://bit.ly/GuardHWife

2. Samantha Johnson, "When I Became A Mother, Feminism Let Me Down," *HuffPost,* February 8, 2017, archived URL: http://bit.ly/FemLetDown

> In the fight to ensure equality, as we preach to girls that they can — and should — do anything a boy can do, we are failing to prepare women for one of the greatest challenges so many of them will face: motherhood. We are teaching our young people that there is no value in motherhood and that homemaking is an outdated, misogynistic concept. We do this through the promotion of professional progression as a marker of success, while completely devaluing the contribution of parents in the home.
>
> We then wonder why, when these girls become women who turn into mothers, they suffer from depression, anxiety and struggle to find a sense of self or identity. Are we truly helping women get ahead, or are we instead setting them up for a future of self-doubt and a sense of failure?

Johnson suggests that instead of "perpetuating the myth" that work at home is "less meaningful," being a homemaker should be viewed as being just as important a career option as any other. Young people, in particular, should be taught "how to care for children, how to cook, how to clean and organize, how to manage household budgets and administration."

Social Affairs Editor for *The Telegraph,* John Bingham reveals in his article *Return of the 1950s housewife?* that several young women in Britain "believe a 'woman's place' is in the home and enjoy housework, buying kitchen gadgets and even making cushions."[1]

Bingham quotes Siobhan Freegard, founder of the websites Netmums and Channel Mum, who claims that the younger

---

1. John Bingham, "Return of the 1950s housewife? Young mothers swap careerism for cushions and casseroles," *The Telegraph,* July 2, 2015, archived URL: http://bit.ly/TeleHWife

generation is realizing that the feminist battles for equality and freedom of choice have actually left them with no choice, for now they go to work, often leaving their babies behind, "not because they want to, not because they love their career but because they have to." According to Freegard, they look at the previous generation, "the 'have-it-all' generation" and think "you lot look knackered, it doesn't look like having it all is that great." So many of them are rejecting the stressful lifestyle "involving a successful career, expensive house" and choosing instead to stay at home, accepting a "more traditional" lifestyle.

Drawing similar conclusions as Bingham and Freegard, Brisbane-based writer Laura Venuto discusses the aspirations of young women in their 20s, the daughters of the trailblazing feminists, who "want nothing more than a happy marriage and domestic bliss in the countryside."[1] Australian women, who have the flexibility to choose between "career, family or a juggling act of both" are reverting to a more traditional role: "The seductive appeal of cooking, housekeeping and family is increasingly favoured by women tired of pushing the boundaries of an ever-present glass ceiling." Several 23-year old women are forgoing a career outside the home and are busy "baking, crocheting, gardening, marrying, procreating, making their own pasta and having Tupperware parties."

Venuto states that while the young women are better educated than their counterparts of the 1950s, and have no desire to reverse changes such as increasing equality at the workplace or at home, they are "stridently rejecting the superwoman model

1. Laura Venuto, "The Return of the Happy Housewife?" *Notebook*, July, 2009, archived URL: http://bit.ly/HappyHWife

of the previous generation." They have practically seen their mothers, or other older women at their workplace, struggle and stress, and finally fail to achieve the balance between career and family, and are anxious to avoid it. In addition, writings such as Virginia Haussegger, who blamed the feminist movement for misguiding women into delaying motherhood until it was too late, warn against falling into the same trap. As a result, the younger generation is rethinking the model of 'career first, family later' and trying to come up with their own hybrid model where they are turning back to traditional roles of being housewives and full-time mothers, with the possibility of returning to part-time work or working from home once the children are older.

In her article *The Retro Wife. Feminists who say they're having it all — by choosing to stay home,* American journalist Lisa Miller observes that women are questioning the feminist notion that housework is abject drudgery and having a career is the only possibility of achieving fulfillment in life.

> Reading *The Feminine Mystique* now, one is struck by the white-hot flame of Betty Friedan's professional hunger, which made her into a prophet and a pioneer. But it blinded her as well: She presumed that all her suburban-housewife sisters felt as imprisoned as she did and that the gratification she found in her work was attainable for all. That was never true, of course; the revolution that Friedan helped to spark both liberated women and allowed countless numbers of them to experience financial pressure and the profound dissatisfactions of the workaday grind. More women than ever earn some or all of the money their family lives on. But today, in the tumultuous 21st-

> century economy, depending on a career as a path to self-actualization can seem like a sucker's bet.[1]

According to Miller, more women opting to be housewives is not just a result of the desire to avoid the stress of juggling work and home, but "a more active awakening to the virtues of the way things used to be." The educated young housewives today are not the frustrated ladies described by Friedan.

> In Friedan's day, housewives used novel technologies such as the automatic washing machine to ease the burden of their domestic work; today, technology helps them to avoid the isolation of their grandmothers and to show off the fruits of their labor. Across the Internet, on a million mommy blogs and Pinterest pages, these women — conceptual cousins of the bearded and suspendered artisanal bakers and brewers who reside in gentrified neighborhoods — are elevating homemaking to an art, crocheting baby hats, slow-roasting strawberries for after-school snacks ("taste like Twizzlers!"), and making their own laundry soap from scratch. Young mothers fill the daytime upholstery and pattern-making courses at Third Ward, a craftspace in Williamsburg, and take knitting classes at the Brooklyn Yarn Café in Bushwick while their kids are in school.
>
> Home, to these women, is more than a place to watch TV at the end of the day and motherhood more than a partial identity. It is a demanding, full-time endeavor, requiring all of their creativity, energy, and ingenuity.

---

1. Lisa Miller, "The Retro Wife. Feminists who say they're having it all — by choosing to stay home," *New York,* March 17, 2013, archived URL: http://bit.ly/RetroWife

Commenting on Miller's article, author of *Homeward Bound: The New Cult of Domesticity*, Emily Matchar writes in *The Altantic:*

> Across different social and cultural groups, there's been a collective return to domesticity — the rise in educated stay-at-home moms, the obsession with traditional crafts, the mania for cooking and growing our own food, the decline in career ambition and the growing importance of family among the young. This phenomenon is about far more than privileged women choosing to stay at home with their children. It's about the laid-off office worker who opens an Etsy boutique selling crocheted baby clothes rather than jumping back into the fray of recession-era job searching. It's about the grown child of harried Baby Boomers who, having seen his parents work 60-hour weeks to climb the corporate ladder, decides to lead a slower, more home-focused life. It's about the young parents who, freaked out about BPA in baby food and pesticides in fruit, decide to take food into their own hands by growing their own veggies and baking their own bread, maybe even raising a chicken or two in the backyard.[1]

During her research, Matchar came across "a wide variety of people" from diverse backgrounds choosing "a different way of life" — young people in Western Pennsylvania attempting to have a lifestyle of self-sufficiency on the land, women in Midwestern America aiming to "revive lost domestic arts like knitting, embroidery, and woodworking" and a large number of working-class women who, in the interest of raising "smarter,

1. Emily Matchar, "The Complex, Often Idealistic Reasons Feminists Become Housewives," *The Atlantic*, March 20, 2013, archived URL: http://bit.ly/Fem2HWife

healthier, gentler children," had "given up full-time jobs — often at great financial cost to their families — in order to breastfeed their babies on demand and carry them in slings." Such people are stepping out of the rat race to adopt a more peaceful, family-oriented way of life. Matchar concludes:

> What they shared was a conviction that America was messed up, and that all-out careerism and materialist values weren't working anymore. They believed that a different way of life — a slower, more handmade, more family-focused life — was the key to happier, more sustainable future.

Whimsical Oscillation

Śrīla Prabhupāda explains that when a person's primary concern is his own material comfort, he tends to switch from one position to another.

> Material engagement means accepting a particular status for some time and then changing it. This position of changing back and forth is technically known as *bhoga-tyāga*, which means a position of alternating sense enjoyment and renunciation.[1]

This means that we may indulge in a particular activity for some time, then being disappointed in the results, we may give it up. But in the future, we may take it up again. In this way, without proper understanding, one may whimsically oscillate from one position to another.

1. His Divine Grace A.C. Bhaktivedanta Swami Prabhupāda, *Nectar of Devotion. The Complete Science of Bhakti-Yoga* (Mumbai, India: The Bhaktivedanta Book Trust, 2011), Preface, xiii.

The past century has seen considerable "back and forth" regarding women's role in the western world. Women began to question their traditional role in the early twentieth century. Yet, post World War II, they were inspired to again embrace the role of the homemaker;[1] thus began the baby boom era. That period lasted until the second wave of feminism sparked by activists such as Betty Friedan led them to renounce their domestic duties. The back and forth continues to the current day with the present generation contemplating yet another role reversal by going back to being housewives instead of career women. However, even if this trend is successful, if followed without the proper understanding, there is a high probability that a few decades down the line, women will again protest against their homebound role.

If we allow ourselves to be solely dictated by personal sense enjoyment and base our decisions on our practical experience of the recent past, we are likely to endlessly fluctuate from one position to another.

However, when conventional experience is coupled with wisdom from the scriptures, we arrive at a model which is not just based on social and psychological factors, but also takes into account the spiritual needs of individuals. With this understanding, a revival of traditional values will not just be a knee-jerk reaction to work-related stress, but will be a sustainable way of life for generations to come.

1. "In the fifteen years after the Second World War, this mystique of feminine fulfilment became the cherished and self-perpetuating core of contemporary American culture. [...] [American women] pitied their poor frustrated mothers, who had dreamed of having a career. They glorified in their role as women, and wrote proudly on the census blank: 'Occupation: housewife'." (Friedan, *The Feminine Mystique*, 8).

Rebelling Against the Rebels

In the modern age, every generation seems to go through a phase where they rebel against social tradition and try to carve a niche of their own, but perhaps women of my generation were particularly radical. We were the trailblazers who entered the workforce and experienced the power of being financially independent of our parents or our potential spouse. Many young ladies went abroad to study and settled there for good. Others landed jobs with multinational companies and bought their own house before they were 30. The previously rare phenomena of being a working woman was here to stay for good, and women were reveling in the freedom it granted them. It was liberating to be able to leave the house in the morning, leaving the hired help, and/or mother or mother-in-law to deal with the housework, and instead be engaged in more important things such as attending meetings, giving presentations, and preparing reports.

However, when I was working, I looked at the women on the higher rungs and was not inspired by what I saw. Although their official stance was to promote gender equality at every level, privately they admitted to constantly being under stress, feeling physically tired, hating the daily commute, and particularly feeling guilty and dissatisfied about not being able to spend enough time with their children. One of them told me that her heart sinks at the thought of summer vacations because her children expect to wake up late and lounge around at home, but instead she has to bundle them off, protesting and grumbling, to various summer camps, one after the other, so that she can come to work. Others shared their distress at leaving sick children at home to meet deadlines at work. Even weekends and vacations seemed packed, trying to catch up with chores, spending time with their spouse, and socializing with extended family and friends. Many of them told me that they had no time for themselves.

Virginia Woolf asserted that "a woman must have money and a room of her own" to rise to her creative potential, but in achieving the former, women now had no time to spend in the latter.

I wondered that if these women were harassed about finding the balance between work and home, how would I manage, for in my case the time required for my personal devotional practice and my desire to share it with others was an added component in the entire equation.

Another thing that added to my disillusionment was the fact that although I was in my early twenties I felt more like a middle-aged woman. Not only was I suffering the occupational hazard of being a computer programmer – a bad back – but every few weeks what would start out as a minor cold or cough would become a full-blown infection with fever and accompanying weakness. After being fed-up with popping pills, I spent several months visiting people offering alternative medicine, but nothing seemed to help. The same air-conditioned office that had once seemed like the epitome of comfort now appeared to suffocate me. My colleagues agreed that the combination of erratic meals, exposure to pollution during the commute, and the strain of maintaining their balancing act was telling on their health. Many of them had similar health issues ranging from migraine headaches, gastric problems, to asthma.

I felt that our well-meaning moms, who insisted that we must have careers, had no idea of how challenging that would become. For one thing, the work environment itself has changed considerably over the years. While corporates today claim to be more employee-friendly and flexible than before, the need to stay ahead of the competition inevitably translates into increased workload and stress. Also, it's common for people to relocate for better job opportunities. All these factors have not made it any easier for women who have lost the support of rapidly dissolving large families and communities and at the same time are grappling with increased work pressure.

And so, I opted out.

At that time I was not aware of even 1% of the related research as I am now, but my growing faith in the Vedic view of women, my gut feeling, and my partner's encouragement were enough for me to make this commonsensical decision.

I looked back on the wonderfully happy childhood that I had, recognized the important part that my mom had played in making it happen, and decided that I wanted the same for my children. I wanted to be there, bright and cheerful and rested, to welcome my husband when he came home from work. I wanted to be there for my parents-in-law and parents when they were ailing. I wanted to have a clutter-free, clean and comfortable house. I wanted time to study Vedic scriptures, to chant the Holy Name and to meditate on the meaning of life. I wanted space to do my own thing, and at the same time, to be there for my family.

What I did not expect was the extent of the backlash I received from my peers. Many ladies — on hearing that I had a postgraduate degree in computer engineering from one of the best schools in India and a well-respected job with a multinational engineering firm – couldn't fathom why I would voluntarily choose to stay at home, and were unabashedly scathing in expressing their disdain regarding my decision.

Nevertheless, I stuck to my resolution and I have never regretted it.

Because I had stopped working, we suddenly had the flexibility to travel according to my husband's work requirements. Because I was not working, I was there for all of the doctor's visits when my elder daughter had facial paralysis, and I also had the time to research and give her a fortifying diet in the following months when she was on heavy antibiotic medication. Because I was not working, I could drive to and fro from the hospital for the entire duration that my husband was admitted there after his spontaneous pneumothorax. Because I was not working, I was home to play Legos with my younger daughter, design clothes for her doll and feed her a liquid diet through a straw for weeks after she fell from her cycle and broke her jaw.

But being at home full time is not just about being there when there's a crisis. It's about the seemingly insignificant things that actually matter rather a lot in the long run, like being there when the children get back from school and comforting them if they've been teased or bullied or left out, gladly entertaining friends who drop by unannounced, lending a patient ear to a husband who's fed up with office politics, and giving a hot-water bottle to an elderly parent in the middle of the night to soothe their backache.

Being a SAHM (stay-at-home-mom) means being a manager, gourmet cook, accountant, teacher, counselor, caregiver, event planner, and chauffeuse all rolled into one. One is on call 24/7, 365 days a year, but the perks of the job are unlike any other in the entire world. The people I'm working for and working with are those I love dearly, I have the flexibility to make my workplace as comfortable and aesthetic as I please, I never have to be stressed with workplace politics, and there's no daily commute to get to work. My husband's sigh of happiness when he comes home in the evening, my daughters' shining eyes on the completion of a DIY project, and our giggling fits on lazy afternoons mean more to me than the 'outstanding, fit to be a leader' feedback I had received in my year-end appraisal when I was working.

I'm happy to have rebelled against the rebels.

Conduct

The primary purpose of the *Vedas* is to help people realize their spiritual identity. To aid this understanding, the vast body of the *Vedas* gives clear guidelines on how individuals should regulate their lives. It not only discusses the particular activities a person should engage in according to his propensities, but also defines suitable character traits he should develop in accordance with his duties.

Vedic scriptures acknowledge the power of sex impulse in the lives of all living entities: *puṁsaḥ striyā mithunī-bhāvam etam,* "the attraction between male and female is the basic principle of material existence."[1] It is explained that a woman is like fire and a man like butter — when they come in contact with each other, it is inevitable that the butter will melt.

1. *Śrīmad-Bhāgavatam* 5.5.8.

There are historical accounts of great *yogīs* like Viśvāmitra being distracted from their meditation simply by hearing the ankle bells of a woman. Fierce wars have been fought over a single woman, such as that between *Śrī* Rāma and Rāvaṇa, and even affectionate brothers have killed each other due to their attraction towards the same woman, such as in the case of Sunda and Upasunda fighting over Tilottamā.[1]

While recognizing the power of such sensual attraction, the scriptures further explain that to act on these impulses unrestrictedly is to remain at the level of animals. Human life begins when we enquire about who we really are, and what the purpose of life is — *athāto brahma jijñāsā.*[2] The real purpose of human life is to reestablish our lost connection with God and realize our spiritual identity by engaging in His devotional service. Only such a state will be truly satisfying to the soul.[3] It is explained that although attraction between

---

1. In the *Mahābhārata,* sage Nārada recounts the story of Sunda and Upasunda to caution the Pāṇḍavas against fighting with each other over their common wife, Draupadī: These two brothers were so close to each other that it appeared that they were one individual divided into two parts. On receiving the boon that they may be killed by no one except each other they figured that they were as good as immortal, and proceeded to wreak havoc on the entire universe. At that time, the demigods created an enchantingly beautiful woman named Tilottamā and sent her forth to bewilder the two demons. And so, Sunda and Upasunda's reign of terror came to an abrupt end, for the mere sight of Tilottamā sent them in such a frenzy of lust that they literally fought each to death over her.
2. *Vedānta-sūtra* 1.1.1.
3. *Śrīmad-Bhāgavatam* 1.2.6: "The supreme occupation for all humanity is that by which men can attain to loving devotional service unto the transcendent Lord. Such devotional service must be unmotivated and uninterrupted to completely satisfy the self."

man and woman is the basis of life itself in this world, it simultaneously constitutes bondage that prevents both from advancing spiritually. Thus Vedic civilization recommends restricted interaction between men and women, not just for the purpose of maintaining peace in society by preventing adultery and abuse, but for the higher purpose of allowing both men and women to be in spiritual consciousness, rather than being constantly preoccupied with indulging their desires.

Acceptance of the principle that human life is not meant only for gratifying our senses, practically resulted in both men and women being taught to be self-controlled. Diametrically opposite to current widely-accepted Freudian theory that repression of sexual impulses causes all kinds of mental problems, within the Vedic culture the ability to control one's body and mind was considered to be one of the indications of advancement of civilization. Men and women who freely indulged in intoxication and illicit sex were considered to be uncouth and lived in the forest, away from the cultured society.

Vedic civilization was organized in such a way that it allowed men to fulfill their desires but not be carried away by them. There were four distinct phases of life – *brahmacarya*, *gṛhastha*, *vānaprastha*, and *sannyāsa*, roughly analogous to student life, married life, retirement, and renunciation. Students were trained to be celibate monks until they got married. Because of their training, even as married men they would not look upon their wives simply as objects of unlimited sexual pleasure. Once their children were grown up, they would enter the *vānaprastha* stage in which they would travel to various holy places for months on end and gradually divert their mind away from their family and towards spiritual life. At this stage, husband and wife may be together but would no longer have physical relations. And finally, at the stage of *sannyāsa,* entrusting his wife to the care of his sons, the man would leave his home to completely immerse himself in his spiritual practice. Thus, except for the phase of life from 25 to 50 years of age, men and women would lead lives of celibacy. To facilitate this, the society functioned in a way that would reduce sexual agitation rather than aggravate it.

Admittedly, women have the power to sway the minds of even the most determined men, so in order to maintain purity within the society, the ladies were taught to be shy and restrained. Respecting that the men were trying to control their urges, the women would not behave in a provocative manner.

When Lord *Śrī* Kṛṣṇa was departing from Hastināpura to go back to His kingdom in Dvārakā, the ladies climbed on the rooftops of their palaces to shower flowers on Him and bid Him adieu. Śrīla Prabhupāda comments on their behavior:

> Shyness is a particular extra-natural beauty of the fair sex, and it commands respect from the opposite sex. [...] This incident from the *Mahābhārata* period proves definitely that the ladies of the palace observed strict *pardā* (restricted association with men), and instead of coming down in the open air where Lord Kṛṣṇa and others were assembled, the ladies of the palace went up on the top of the palace and from there paid their respects to Lord Kṛṣṇa by showers of flowers. It is definitely stated here that the ladies were smiling there on the top of the palace, checked by shyness. This shyness is a gift of nature to the fair sex, and it enhances their beauty and prestige, even if they are of

> a less important family or even if they are less attractive. [...] [S]hyness is a check to the unrestricted mixing.[1]

Śrīla Prabhupāda then describes an incident from his youth. He and his friend were standing and talking at the doorway when he noticed that the lady who cleaned their house was standing to one side, waiting for them to give way for she did not want to brush past them to enter the house. He immediately moved aside, impressed by her reluctance to even momentarily come in physical contact with strange men. He writes: "A sweeper woman commanded the respect of many respectable gentlemen simply by manifesting a lady's shyness. Half-naked ladies in the street do not command any respect, but a shy sweeper's wife commands respect from all."[2]

The principle of shyness was not meant to quash the girls' natural exuberance. But the expectation was that while they may be at their vivacious best with their immediate family and close friends, among others they would act in a more dignified way. Here shyness does not refer to being tongue-tied in company. It refers to the quality of not being anxious to flaunt one's assets. For women in Vedic times, this principle was reflected in every aspect of their life, such as their speech, their behavior, and their attire. They were soft-spoken and reticent, not due to their being unsure of themselves or afraid of making a fool of themselves, but because they preferred not to attract attention to themselves. They did not think it necessary to immediately voice their opinion on every matter being discussed. This did not mean that the women's views were not considered at all, just that they were usually content to let the elders take decisions

---

1. *Śrīmad-Bhāgavatam* 1.10.16, purport by Śrīla Prabhupāda.
2. *Śrīmad-Bhāgavatam* 1.10.16, purport by Śrīla Prabhupāda.

and if they wanted to express something, they would do so privately or indirectly through someone else. In the context of a father asking his daughters' preference when selecting a suitable match for them, Śrīla Prabhupāda writes: "Generally the daughters were too shy to express their opinions before their father, but the father would accept the daughters' intentions through someone else, such as a grandmother to whom the grandchildren had free access."[1]

The Vedic women would act demurely, and dress conservatively. They considered that their beauty was only for the pleasure of their husbands, and so did not like to display it publicly. They would be elegantly dressed in a sari, a garment that serves to cover the curves of the body rather than enhance them. Even their long hair would be braided or tied in a bun and then covered with the end of the sari.

Such respectable ladies practiced the virtue of chastity. What to say of indulging in pre-marital sex or extra-marital affairs, these ladies would not even laugh, joke or otherwise behave frivolously with any man, other than their husband. Today, such standards appear to be unnecessarily strict, for people are used to being 'just friends' with members of the opposite sex. However, most affairs (almost all of which eventually lead to wrecking marriages) begin as seemingly innocuous friendships. Therefore, wisely acknowledging the natural sexual tension between men and women, Vedic sages caution women to avoid such so-called platonic relationships with men.

Sexual Revolution: Whom Does It Benefit?

In sharp contrast to Vedic times, today, 'shyness' and 'chastity' are obsolete terms which young ladies are largely unfamiliar

1. *Śrīmad-Bhāgavatam* 3.14.14, purport by Śrīla Prabhupāda.

with. Believing them to be tools used by patriarchy to control women and restrain their sexual activity, feminists fought for women's right to have sex with whomever they wanted, whenever they wanted. Helen Gurley Brown's book *Sex and The Single Girl* (1962), which "encouraged women to become financially independent and experience sexual relationships before or without marriage" sold two million copies in three weeks.[1]

The post-World War II era in particular saw the emergence of an ideology of sexual permissiveness, fueled by rebellion against traditional values and influenced by theories of Sigmund Freud and Alfred Kinsey. The media and entertainment industry further reinforced these ideas, with magazines such as *Playboy* glamorizing recreational sex and pornography. Finally, with the introduction and popularization of the contraceptive pill, the last hurdle towards sexual equality, i.e. women's reluctance to be promiscuous for fear of becoming pregnant, seemed to be removed. The 1960s saw such a radical shift in attitudes towards sexuality and marriage that the phenomenon was termed the 'sexual revolution.'

Currently, a woman may have multiple live-in relationships with a series of men (or women) before making up her mind whether or not she wants to marry, and she will not be ostracized by the society. She can sunbathe at a beach in a bikini and no one will raise an eyebrow. She can have an impulsive one-night stand and still remain carefree by taking advantage of the morning-after pill.

However, half a century after the sexual revolution of the 1960s, people are beginning to question whether sexual freedom has

1. "Sex and the Single Girl," *Wikipedia, the Free Encyclopedia*, last modified 21 January, 2019, archived URL: http://bit.ly/wiki1girl

truly benefited women. While American author Ann Pratchet argues that the sexual revolution has been good for women because it was "not so much a matter of sleeping around as it was of having the ability to decide when you were going to have a child, and then deciding how many children you wanted to have,"[1] British journalist Virginia Ironside disagrees through her recollection of the era of 'free love.' It was a misnomer, Ironside says, that brought about a social system where it was expected that young people would indulge in casual sex with little idea about "how damaging [their] sexual behaviour was both to [their] self-esteem and [their] souls."[2] Ironside writes, "And although I've no doubt it was a fantastic — or 'fab' as we used to say — time for men, for women (or young girls as we were then) it was absolutely grisly. [...] To be honest, I mainly remember the 60s as an endless round of miserable promiscuity, a time when often it seemed easier and, believe it or not, more polite, to sleep with a man than to chuck him out of your flat."

Echoing a similar sentiment, journalist Bel Mooney writes in *My generation created the sexual revolution — and it has been wrecking the lives of women ever since:*

> The university Student Health Centre handed out the Pill like sweeties. So you wouldn't get pregnant — good. But at the same time you had no reason to be careful — bad.

---

1. Ann Patchett, "Has the Sexual Revolution Been Good for Women? Yes," *The Wall Street Journal,* March 30, 2012, archived URL: http://bit.ly/wsjsexrevolt

2. Virginia Ironside, "'We paid the price for free love': The flip side of the sexual revolution," *MailOnline,* January 18, 2011, archived URL: http://bit.ly/DMSexRevolt

> Most of us embraced the hippie-esque idea that sexual freedom was a beautiful thing to be celebrated. 'Seize the day,' we shouted, and threw old notions like fidelity out of the window.
>
> However, the women began to realize that the "high-sounding ideals" promoted by "supposedly radical and free-thinking men" was "insidious" in that it pretended to be an alternative for women, when actually it was providing an alternative for men to engage in sex without facing any consequences.
>
> It was paradise for men — all these willing girls. But the problem with the willing girls was that a lot of the time they were willing not because they particularly fancied the people concerned but because they felt they ought to. There was a lot of misery. [...]
>
> Sex, which in previous eras was private (even taboo), became public, with the result that women were expected — in their love lives — to demonstrate the expertise of prostitutes. Except these 'liberated' women gave it away for free. [...]
>
> The sad thing is young women today are still being conned — victims of the pervasive sex industry which uses 'liberation' as a mask for degradation.[1]

Psychologist Nigel Barber questions whether it is the women or men who have benefited from women's sexual liberation. He writes:

---

1. Bel Mooney, "My generation created the sexual revolution — and it has been wrecking the lives of women ever since." *The Daily Mail,* December 2, 2009, archived URL: http://bit.ly/SexWreak

> Whereas men are generally more interested in casual sex, women look for greater emotional commitment in a relationship. [...] From an evolutionary perspective, the so-called sexual liberation of women looks more like sexual liberation for men, i.e. men get more sex and more sexual variety without making an emotional commitment.
>
> Because they are over-supplied and less in demand, women enter into the spirit of men's penchant for recreational sex. This psychology is at an extreme on U.S. college campuses where there are only about 75 men per hundred women and hooking up (some level of physical intimacy that lasts for just one night) has largely replaced dating. As women's bargaining power declines, they must behave more like men if they wish to remain active in the romantic sphere. Women certainly gain in sexual freedom compared to their grandmothers but they lose out in emotional commitment.[1]

Author of *Adam and Eve After the Pill: Paradoxes of the Sexual Revolution,* Mary Eberstadt suggests that it's a myth that the sexual revolution has made women happier:

> Granted, happiness is a personal, imponderable thing. But if the sexual revolution has really made women as happy as feminists say, a few elementary questions beg to be answered.
>
> Why do the pages of our tonier magazines brim with mournful titles like "The Case for Settling" and "The End of Men"? Why do websites run by and for women focus so much on men who won't grow up, and ooze such despair about relations between the sexes?

1. Nigel Barber, "Sexual liberation: Whose sexuality is liberated, men's or women's?" *Psychology Today,* April 14, 2009, archived URL: http://bit.ly/SexLib

> Why do so many accomplished women simply give up these days and decide to have children on their own, sometimes using anonymous sperm donors, thus creating the world's first purposely fatherless children? What of the fact, widely reported, that over a quarter of American women are on some kind of mental-health medication for anxiety and depression and related problems?[1]

American writer Pearl Buck predicted the effect of the contraceptive pill in 1968, in a *Reader's Digest* article: "Everyone knows what The Pill is. It is a small object — yet its potential effect upon our society may be even more devastating than the nuclear bomb."[2] Eberstadt elaborates:

> In severing sex from procreation, humankind set into motion forces that have by now shaped and reshaped almost every aspect of life in the Western world. Families are smaller, birthrates have dropped, divorce and out-of-wedlock births have soared. Demography has now even started to work against the modern welfare state, which has become harder to sustain as fewer children have been produced to replace aging parents. The sexual revolution has transformed economics, culture and law.[3]

By demanding that women should have the right to engage in physical relations with a man without any strings attached, the feminists certainly created a culture in which women can satisfy their desires without being criticized by the society

---

1. Mary Eberstadt, "Has the Sexual Revolution Been Good for Women? No," *The Wall Street Journal,* March 20, 2012, archived URL: http://bit.ly/SexRevNoGood
2. Pearl Buck, "The Pill and the Teenage Girl," *Reader's Digest* 92, no. 552 (April 1968).
3. Eberstadt, "Sexual Revolution."

(Cyndi Lauper's song *Girls Just Wanna Have Fun*[1] came to be widely accepted as a feminist anthem); they have greater control over their lives and have the ability to postpone, or avoid, having children in the interest of pursuing a career. But the same culture has also opened the door to easy exploitation of women, and degraded the position of women to that of sex objects for casual enjoyment. At the present time, the mainstream media is full of images of women which, a few decades ago, would have only been seen in the centerfold of a censored men's-only magazine. Similarly, the movies and entertainment shows on TV routinely depict graphic scenes which can be classified as soft porn.

Hookup Culture: Strings Attached to the 'No strings attached' Culture

A legacy of the 'revolution' that started decades ago was that it was considered perfectly normal for a man and woman to be physically intimate before they are in a committed relationship, instead of the other way round. And it did not stop there — not only would sex be separated from marriage, it would progressively be separated from anything resembling a relationship.

Commenting on life in America at the turn of the century, author of *Hooking Up* Tom Wolfe observes: "If anything, 'sexual revolution' was rather a prim term for the lurid carnival actually taking place in the mightiest country on earth in the year 2000."[2] He described how the media, in the form of magazines and later the Internet, bombarded people

1. Cyndi Lauper, "Girls Just Wanna Have Fun," on *She's So Unusual*, Portrait Records, 1983, compact disk.

2. Tom Wolfe, *Hooking Up* (New York: Picador USA, 2000), 5.

with sex-related content to such an extent that "the word 'perversion' had become as obsolete as 'pornography'" for the terms they represented had become so commonplace that one hardly paid much attention to them. This cultural onslaught has powerfully permeated the relationships and attitudes of people in general:

> "Sexy" was beginning to replace "chic" as the adjective indicating what was smart and up-to-the-minute. In the year 2000, it was standard practice for the successful chief executive officer of a corporation to shuck his wife of two to three decades' standing for the simple reason that her subcutaneous packing was deteriorating, her shoulders and upper back were thickening like a shot-putter's — in short, she was no longer sexy. Once he set up the old wife in a needlepoint shop where she could sell yarn to her friends, he was free to take on a new wife, a "trophy wife," preferably a woman in her twenties, and preferably blond, as in an expression from that time, a "lemon tart."[1]

For the young people, the concept of 'dating' was replaced with that of 'hookups' — physical intimacy with no strings attached.

> In the nineteenth century, entire shelves used to be filled with novels whose stories turned on the need for women, such as Anna Karenina or Madame Bovary, to remain chaste or to maintain a façade of chastity. In the year 2000, a Tolstoy or a Flaubert wouldn't have stood a chance in the United States. From age thirteen, American girls were under pressure to maintain a façade of sexual experience and sophistication. Among girls, "virgin" was a term of contempt. The old term "dating" — referring to a practice in which a boy asked a girl out for the evening and took her to

1. Ibid., 6.

> the movies or dinner — was now deader than "proletariat" or "pornography" or "perversion." In junior high school, high school, and college, girls headed out in packs in the evening, and boys headed out in packs, hoping to meet each other fortuitously. If they met and some girl liked the looks of some boy, she would give him the nod, or he would give her the nod, and the two of them would retire to a halfway-private room and "hook up."[1]

In the two decades since Wolfe wrote the above article, there has been considerable discussion regarding the 'hookup culture,' particularly in relation to its prevalence on college campuses in America.

In her book *Hooking Up: Sex, Dating, and Relationships on Campus* Kathleen A. Bogle divides the last century into three distinct periods — the calling era, the dating era and the hookup era. In the calling era, in the early twentieth century, a young man may "call" on or visit a young lady he was interested in, at her house, under the supervision of her parents.[2] Next came the dating era, in the period from 1920s to 1960s, when young couples in romantic relationships "began going out, away from the watchful eyes of parents"[3] and "increasing sexual intimacy entered the equation."[4] Finally, the hookup era, or the period of casual sex began in the 1960s with sexual liberalization and the feminist movement, when it was no longer considered necessary to be in a relationship to have sexual relations with someone. Bogle writes:

---

1. Ibid., 6.
2. Kathleen A. Bogle, *Hooking Up: Sex, Dating, and Relationships on Campus* (New York: New York University Press, 2008), 12.
3. Ibid., 13.
4. Ibid., 19.

> This shift away from traditional dating was particularly apparent on college campuses. College students began socializing in groups, rather than pair dating, and "partying" with a large number of friends and classmates. Parties represented more than just a social outing; they became the setting for potential sexual encounters.[1]

As the culture evolved, this, in fact, was to become the norm, rather than an option. As Donna Freitas explains in *The End of Sex: How Hookup Culture is Leaving a Generation Unhappy, Sexually Unfulfilled, and Confused About Intimacy:*

> Hookups have existed throughout human history, of course, but what is now happening on American campuses is something different. College has gone from being a place where hookups happened to a place where hookup culture dominates student attitudes about all forms of intimacy. The hookup has become *normative,* and hookup culture a monolithic culture from which students find little chance of escape. It is the defining aspect of social life on many campuses; to reject it is to relegate oneself to the sidelines of college experience.[2]

In *Unhooked: How Young Women Pursue Sex, Delay Love and Lose at Both,* Laura Sessions Stepp emphasizes that a lack of commitment and emotional involvement is the primary feature of this culture:

> The crucial thing to remember in all of this is that hooking up, in the minds of this generation, carries no

1. Ibid., 20.

2. Donna Freitas, *The End of Sex: How Hookup Culture is Leaving a Generation Unhappy, Sexually Unfulfilled, and Confused About Intimacy* (New York: Basic Books, 2013), 5.

> commitment. Partners hook up with the understanding that however far they go sexually, neither should become romantically involved in any serious way. Hookups defining characteristic is the ability to *unhook* from a partner at any time, just as one might delete an old song from their iPod or an out-of-date "away" message on their computer. Maybe they tire of their partner, or find someone who is "hotter" or, for some other reason, more to their liking.[1]

Justifying the need for such a disposable culture, Matthew Yglesias, the executive editor of *Vox*, promoted casual sex as a "sound option" for college students (whom he describes as "physically mature adults with sexual interests" who "don't want to be virgins until the age of 25"),[2] since it is preferable to being in a serious, committed relationship doomed to fail when the couple part ways after college to pursue their careers. Yglesias elaborates:

> Looking to meet your spouse in college is about as outdated as quitting high school to get a job at the local factory, and for roughly the same reasons. Young people should feel free to do what they want with their sex lives, but I think it's the people who are following neo-traditional visions of dating and romance who are operating with bad information and are more likely in need of guidance.

Echoing *Vox*'s editor, author Hanna Rosin asserts that hookup culture played a key role in making women successful:

---

1. Laura Sessions Stepp, *Unhooked: How Young Women Pursue Sex, Delay Love and Lose at Both* (New York: Riverhead Books, 2007), 5–6.
2. Matthew Yglesias, "Who Will Save College Students From The Scourge of Doomed Campus Relationships?" *Slate*, July 16, 2013, archived URL: http://bit.ly/HookupCult

> Single young women in their sexual prime — that is, their 20s and early 30s, the same age as the women at the business-school party — are for the first time in history more successful, on average, than the single young men around them. They are more likely to have a college degree and, in aggregate, they make more money. What makes this remarkable development possible is not just the pill or legal abortion but the whole new landscape of sexual freedom — the ability to delay marriage and have temporary relationships that don't derail education or career. To put it crudely, feminist progress right now largely depends on the existence of the hookup culture. And to a surprising degree, it is women — not men — who are perpetuating the culture, especially in school, cannily manipulating it to make space for their success, always keeping their own ends in mind. For college girls these days, an overly serious suitor fills the same role an accidental pregnancy did in the 19th century: a danger to be avoided at all costs, lest it gets in the way of a promising future.[1]

The New York Times' reporter, Kate Taylor's observation about women at University of Pennsylvania choosing 'hookups' over dating runs along similar lines. She writes in her well-known article *Sex on Campus: She Can Play That Game, Too:*

> These women said they saw building their résumés, not finding boyfriends (never mind husbands), as their main job at Penn. They envisioned their 20s as a period of unencumbered striving, when they might work at a bank in Hong Kong one year, then go to business school, then move to a corporate job in New York. The idea of lugging a relationship through all those transitions was hard for

---

1. Hanna Rosin, "Boys on the Side," *The Atlantic,* September 2012, archived URL: http://bit.ly/BoySide

> many to imagine. Almost universally, the women said they did not plan to marry until their late 20s or early 30s.
>
> In this context, some women, like A., seized the opportunity to have sex without relationships, preferring "hookup buddies" (regular sexual partners with little emotional commitment) to boyfriends.[1]

However, this preference for the transitory was not universally true for all the women Taylor interviewed. Some "longed for boyfriends and deeper attachment." But, when they arrived at college, and realized that there's little possibility of forming meaningful relationships, they settled for hooking up while trying not to get attached.

Furthermore, Freitas refutes Rosin's claim that young women are actually better off with the hookup culture and are "cannily manipulating it to make space for their success":

> Rosin's argument is fascinating, but, based on my research, I believe it is also misleading. It is true that the existence of hookup culture allows young women to put off relationships. Yet it doesn't simply *allow* this, it fairly *forbids* the formation of long-term romantic attachments, something both genders complain about in private. It is also true that women perpetuate the culture (just as men do), but young women say they feel they have no option. The same students who talk approvingly of hookup culture in certain settings (say, at a party, or in front of their friends in the dorms) will often denounce it in anonymous surveys or private personal interviews.[2]

1. Kate Taylor, "Sex on Campus: She Can Play That Game, Too," *The New York Times*, July 12, 2013, archived URL: http://bit.ly/CampuSex
2. Freitas, *End of Sex*, 8-9.

Freitas' observation that women are drawn into the culture as if "they have no option" is supported by Nancy Jo Sales' article in *Vanity Fair*, an investigation into the effect of websites like Tinder, which are allegedly dating sites but in reality facilitate hooking up. Seniors from Boston College shared their dissatisfaction with Sales, but at the same time indicated that they were reluctant to question it so as to avoid being the odd one out:

> "It seems like the girls don't have any control over the situation, and it should not be like that at all," Fallon says.
>
> "It's a contest to see who cares less, and guys win a lot at caring less," Amanda says.
>
> "Sex should stem from emotional intimacy, and it's the opposite with us right now, and I think it really is kind of destroying females' self-images," says Fallon.
>
> "It's body first, personality second," says Stephanie.
>
> "Honestly, I feel like the body doesn't even matter to them as long as you're willing," says Reese. "It's that bad."
>
> "But if you say any of this out loud, it's like you're weak, you're not independent, you somehow missed the whole memo about third-wave feminism," says Amanda.[1]

Freitas confirms that most people feel impelled to conform:

> I've spent the past eight years investigating hookup culture and talking with students, faculty members and college administrators about it. I thought I would find that the vast

1. Nancy Jo Sales, "Tinder and the Dawn of the "Dating Apocalypse"," *Vanity Fair*, September 2015, archived URL: http://bit.ly/VanityCult

> majority of students revel in it, but instead I encountered a large percentage who feel confined by it or ambivalent about it (the "whateverists," as I call them). Nervous to be alone in challenging hookup culture, most students go along with it, even if they privately long for alternatives. They think that if they try to be less casual about sex, it'll ruin their social lives. Conformity abounds.[1]

This insidious social dynamic is now so pervasive that almost everyone is inexorably drawn into it. Yet, whether they are enthusiastically embracing it or are reluctant participants, the hookup culture, although promising to provide pleasure, is often the cause of bewilderment and unhappiness. Freitas writes: "Of students who reported hooking up, 41 percent used words such as 'regretful,' 'empty,' 'miserable,' 'disgusted,' 'ashamed,' 'duped' and even 'abused' to describe the experience."

Leah Fessler is a writer based in New York City, and also a graduate from prestigious Middlebury College in Vermont. Influenced by writings of Hanna Rosin and Kate Taylor, Fessler found herself an enthusiastic participant of the hookup culture while at Middlebury College:

> I soon came to believe that real relationships were impossible at Midd. I convinced myself I didn't want one anyway. It wasn't just the social pressure that drove me to buy into the commitment-free hookup lifestyle, but my own identity as a feminist. The idea that sexual liberation is fundamental to female agency dominates progressive media. True feminists, I believed, not only

1. Donna Freitas, "Time to stop hooking up. (You know you want to.)" *The Washington Post,* March 29, 2013, archived URL: http://bit.ly/StopHookup

> wanted but also thrived on emotionless, non-committal sexual engagements. [...] I decided it was time to ditch my antiquated desire for monogamy. As Taylor's article suggested, I would "play the game, too."[1]

However, soon Fessler was forced to accept that it was impossible to have physical relations and not have any feelings attached to it: "With time, inevitably, came attachment. And with attachment came shame, anxiety, and emptiness." She observed that it was the same with all her other friends — although they accepted the culture, they were hurt by the "unspoken social code" that "neither party is permitted emotional involvement, commitment, or vulnerability." She concluded: "If this was sexual liberation, it was hard to understand how it was helping women."

Fessler was so disturbed by the entire experience that she devoted her senior thesis to answering the question about hookup culture at Middlebury. She found that "100% of female interviewees and three-quarters of female survey respondents stated a clear preference for committed relationships" and only "8% of about 25 female respondents who said they were presently in pseudo-relationships reported being 'happy' with their situation." Fessler writes:

> My research gave me a sense of solace. Most Middlebury women were "playing the game," yet almost none of us enjoyed it. I went on to publish my thesis online, and stories from students around the country came pouring in. It was clear we were far from alone.

1. Leah Fessler, "A lot of women don't enjoy hookup culture — so why do we force ourselves to participate?" *Quartz,* May 17, 2016, archived URL: http://bit.ly/UnlikeHookup

In her book *American Hookup: The New Culture of Sex on Campus*, Lisa Wade comments on this phenomenon:

> On campuses across America, students are sounding an alarm. They are telling us that they are depressed, anxious and overwhelmed. Half of first-year students express concern that they are not emotionally healthy, and one in ten say they are frequently depressed. The transition from teenagers to young adult is rarely easy, but this is more than just youthful angst. Students are less happy and healthy than in previous generations, less so even than just ten or twenty years ago. [...]
>
> One in three students say that their intimate relationships have been "traumatic" or "very difficult to handle," and 10 percent say they have been sexually coerced or assaulted in the past year. In addition, there is a persistent malaise: a deep, indefinable disappointment. [...] They are frustrated and feel regret, but they're not sure why.[1]

The cause of the students' unhappiness, according to Wade, is the hookup culture, which has descended like inclement weather with limited visibility:

> Hookup culture is an occupying force, coercive and omnipresent. For those who love it, it's all sunshine, but it isn't for everyone else. Deep in the fog, students often feel dreary, confused, helpless. Many behave in ways they don't like, hurt other people unwillingly, and consent to sexual activity they don't desire.
>
> Campuses of all kinds are in this fog. No matter the size of the college, how heavy a Greek or athletic presence it

---

1. Lisa Wade, *American Hookup: The New Culture of Sex on Campus* (New York: W. W. Norton & Company, Inc., 2017), 15.

> boasts, its exclusivity, its religious affiliation, or whether it's public or private, hookup culture is there. [...]
>
> In response many students opt out of hooking up, but they can't opt out of hookup culture. Its more than just a behavior; it's the climate. It can't be wished away any more than we can wish away a foggy day.[1]

Wade suggests that the hookup culture be taken seriously and its consequences discussed, for it is indicative not just of what is happening at college campuses, but of the mood that is pervading society in general:

> The fog, in other words, isn't just on college campuses; it's everything. [...] We need to understand what's happening on college campuses because what's happening there is happening everywhere.[2]

Not only is the culture psychologically damaging to the young people, there is a dangerous edge to it which threatens their safety, as described by the students at Penn — "sexual assaults and degrading encounters enabled by drinking and distinguished by a lack of emotional connection."[3] They all unanimously agreed that "hookups could not exist without alcohol because they were for most part too uncomfortable to pair off with men they did not know well without being drunk." The women shared disturbing experiences of coercion and abuse, and explained that whenever drinking was involved the men automatically assumed that the girls were willing to engage in just about anything, and so they would not hesitate to take advantage of them.

1. Ibid., 19-20.
2. Ibid., 25.
3. Kate Taylor, "Sex on Campus."

Commenting on Lisa Wade's book, Sezín Koehler observes: "Disturbingly, hookup culture also effectively allows sexual predators to hide in plain sight since their criminal activity might be indistinguishable from some of hookup culture's ugly but acceptable behaviors."[1] Like Fessler, Koehler too failed to see how a culture that leads to "the degradation and sexual objectification of women" could ever be accepted as a "feminist act." She concludes: "It seems to me that opting *out* of hookup culture would be the more powerful and rebellious political statement a person could make."

People like Yglesias are advocates of consent-based sexual morality, which means that there should be no objection to two people engaging in sex as long as both individuals are adults and consent to it. They claim that this concept allows individuals to express themselves more freely since it removes the social stigmatization of someone who indulges in sex outside of marriage. However, according to writer David French, it creates larger problems of its own:

> The practical result of consent-focused morality is the sexualization of everything. With the line drawn at desire alone, there is no longer any space that's sex-free. Work meetings or restaurants can be creative locations for steamy liaisons. Not even marriage or existing relationships stand as a firewall against potential hookups. [...] Desire is elevated over fidelity and certainly over propriety, so bosses bully, spouses stray, hearts break, and families fracture.
>
> It virtually goes without saying that the sex drive is incredibly powerful. Sex is also a remarkably intimate

1. Sezín Koehler, "The Sociology Of Casual Sexual Encounters With Lisa Wade," *HuffPost*, last updated February 14, 2018, archived URL: http://bit.ly/SoCasual

> act that often has a profound emotional impact. An ethic that indulges that drive while also denying the emotional significance of sex will inevitably wreck lives. The wise person understands that desire — even mutual desire — can be dangerous.[1]

French also points out that it allows men in power to easily manipulate women, particularly those under their authority. *The New York Times* columnist Ross Douthat agrees, pointing out that consent-based morality needs to be reexamined not only because of the predation it encourages, but due to the simple fact that it has not made people in general happier.

> In a world of consent and assumed promiscuity, the predator plays on the idea that sex isn't such a big deal, that what he's asking for is really a small thing, that you should be a good sport and play along and if you're offended or hurt or feel that you've been violated, well look we're all adults here and again, it's just sex, it's transactional and ephemeral, an exchange of pleasures so why not an exchange of pleasure for a job, and I'm sorry that my pursuit of self-fulfillment didn't quite respect your boundaries, but since I didn't rape you and maybe you led me on, you don't have any grounds for complaint [...]
>
> In certain ways I think the mess on college campuses — not the clearly-rape cases, not the Hefnerite excesses of frat culture[2] (which a stronger feminism might eventually

---

1. David French, "It's Past Time to Rethink Modern Sexual Morality," *National Review,* October 15, 2017, archived URL: http://bit.ly/SexConsentMoral

2. Hugh Hefner, through the publication of *Playboy* and his own lifestyle, was instrumental in promoting a culture that objectifies women as sexual objects meant to be enjoyed by men.

> restrain), but the endless gray-zone drunk-sex cases at the most self-consciously progressive schools — tells us more about the inherent problems with "consent alone" than does the mess in Hollywood, because it's a case where there's more social equality, less boss-on-minion pressure, and a generally sex-positive culture of experimentation [...] and yet young people still clearly desire and need a system of rules stronger than consent alone to protect them from feeling unexpected rage or shame over how a particular encounter happened.
>
> But really the strongest evidence is rather less dramatic than the extremes of rape and assault, predation and harassment. It lies in the fact that our consenting-adults moral system isn't serving what should be the obvious ends of any moral-sexual ecosystem: To make people happy, to make women happy, to successfully balance the often very different sexual/romantic impulses of the sexes, to pair off as many people as wish to be paired off as contentedly as possible in ways that ensure stable environments for their children to flourish, and to encourage the continuation of present societies and the human race.[1]

As Douthat comments regarding college students, the problem with consent-based sexual morality is that when the individuals in question are young adults, they may not even be aware of the consequences of their consent and, in truth, need protection in the form of stricter rules, rather than a free-for-all.

Ironically, instead of stricter rules, the universities are competing with each other to be more liberal. Professors Vigen Guroian and William Wilson hold the universities responsible

---

1. Ross Douthat, "The Age of Consent and Its Discontents," *The New York Times*, October 19, 2017, archived URL: http://bit.ly/ConsentAge

in part for the moral decline. They describe how things changed when, under the influence of the sexual revolution, colleges went from being single-sex institutes to unisex, and the authorities gave tacit encouragement to the students to experiment.

> Back then, we were told that the old order must be abolished because the standards and conventions it embodied favored men. Young women would be sexually liberated and the "playing field" leveled. Therefore, parietal hours were eliminated and mixed-sex dorms, once inconceivable, became the norm. In the process, the new unisex coeducational colleges and universities that are so familiar to us today came into existence.[1]

They quote an alumna of University of Virginia to describe the dismal state of affairs today:

> Sexual license was actively encouraged and funded by the university. From "Spring-break fun packs" full of condoms and forms of contraception handed out at the student center with a cute note from a pudgy sunshine face wearing shades saying "Have a Fun Spring Break!" to "Sexual Arts and Crafts" flyers plastered on the dorm halls — the message is clear: college is a parent-funded motel party of casual and impersonal, but, yes, "safe sex."

The sad truth is that the hookup culture is not just restricted to American college campuses. It is seen at the workplace, and in college campuses and high schools all over the world. Young

---

1. Vigen Guroian and William Wilson, "Sex and Danger at UVA. An Argument for the University's Complicity in the Destructive Culture of Sex," *First Things*, March 2015, archived URL: http://bit.ly/UVADanger

people have come to expect college life to have an abundance of three things: sex, drugs and rock and roll.

When my sister was considering joining the distinguished Jawaharlal Nehru University in Delhi, we went there to meet with the daughter of one of my father's acquaintances. While my parents were busy enquiring about the admission procedure, my sister, coming from a small town and familiar with the university's reputation for being liberal, curiously asked the young girl, "Do you smoke?" She looked us straight in the eye and replied meaningfully, "In JNU, *everyone* smokes." My sister would soon discover that that's not all that everyone does. This was more than twenty years ago. Today no one would be naïve enough to ask such a question, even of school children in Delhi, what to say of college students. There seems to be a strange paradox that the more prestigious an educational institute is, the more degraded the moral standard on its campus is.

Four leading psychologists prepared an extensive report[1] to review the impact of hookup culture on society. Their research highlighted that although both men and women had negative reactions to hookups, women were affected to a greater degree. "The percentage of women expressing guilt was more than twice that of men" and "in deliberate hookup situations women had more thoughts of worry and vulnerability than men." Women's "degree of depressive symptoms increased with number of previous sex partners within the last year," and those who "engaged in an uncommitted sexual encounter had lower overall self-esteem scores." In a study concerning one-night stands, it became evident that "both men and women

1. Justin R. Garcia et al., "Sexual Hookup Culture: A Review," *Review of General Psychology* 16, no. 2 (2012): 161–176.

had experienced some sexual regret," but the "frequency and intensity of negative reactions" was greater for women as "they felt used." Their research also underlined the darker side of the culture: "Not all hookup encounters are necessarily wanted or consensual." In several studies "participants noted that a majority of their unwanted sex occurred in the context of hookups."

The psychologists concluded that although "hookups provide the allure of sex without strings attached," actually they "may leave more strings attached than many participants might first assume."[1]

What Happened to the Age of Innocence?

What is particularly alarming about the 'hookup culture' is that it is not limited to the universities alone. It has progressively seeped into schools, affected teenagers, and pre-teens as well. It's bad enough when young children indulge in sexual activity, but it's exponentially worse when they do so in the cold, emotionless way that hookup culture dictates.

According to a report published by Center of Disease Control, in United States, "In 2011–2015, 42.4% of never-married female teenagers (4.0 million) and 44.2% of never-married male teenagers (4.4 million) had had sexual intercourse at least once by the time of the interview (were sexually experienced)."[2]

1. Justin R. Garcia et al., "Sexual hook-up culture," *American Psychological Association,* February 2013, archived URL: http://bit.ly/SexHookCult

2. Joyce C. Abma and Gladys M. Martinez, "Sexual Activity and Contraceptive Use Among Teenagers in the United States, 2011–2015," *National Health Statistics Reports,* no. 104 (June 22, 2017), archived URL: http://bit.ly/TeenContraceptives

A research paper published in the medical journal *Acta Paediatrica* that examined the effect of sexual debut before the age of 14 on psychosocial health and risky behaviour in later life, concluded "Early debut was positively correlated with risky behaviours, such as the number of partners, experience of oral and anal sex, health behaviours, such as smoking, drug and alcohol use, and antisocial behaviour, such as being violent, lying, stealing and running away from home. Girls with an early sexual debut had significantly more experience of sexual abuse."[1]

A study sponsored by the Centers for Disease Control of the U.S. Department of Health and Human Services examined data from 10,000 women between the ages of 15 and 44 based on the National Survey of Family Growth. It tabulated the harmful effects of early sexual activity and multiple sexual partners among women, concluding as follows:

> The earlier a woman begins sexual activity, the more sexual partners she is likely to have during her lifetime. Girls who begin voluntary sexual activity at ages 13 or 14 will have, on average, more than 13 voluntary non-marital sex partners during their lives. By contrast, women who begin sexual activity in their early 20s will have, on average, 2.7 sexual partners during their lives. Women who begin sexual activity at early ages also have far higher turnover rates among sexual partners. (The sex partner turnover rate may be defined as the number of sex partners per year of sexual activity.) Women who become sexually active at ages 13–14 have a sex partner turnover rate that is four

1. Asa A. Kastbom et al., "Sexual debut before the age of 14 leads to poorer psychosocial health and risky behaviour in later life," *Acta Paediatrica* 104, no. 1 (January 2015): 91–100.

> times higher than the rate found among those who initiate sex activity in their early 20s.[1]

Further, the report states that early sexual activity "is likely to have permanent negative consequences on the lives of young women" which can be "physical, psychological, social, and economic." Such young girls are more likely to be infected by sexually transmitted diseases, and more likely to become pregnant. As a result, they are more likely to have abortions, give birth out-of-wedlock and become single mothers. Early sexual activity is "linked to higher levels of child and maternal poverty" and it also "seriously undermines girls' ability to form stable marriages as adults." Such girls report lower "personal happiness" than those who begin sexual activity in early 20s. Similar negative impacts, such as increased probability of being infected by sexually transmitted infections, being single mothers, having abortions, etc., were also apparent for women who have an increased number of non-marital sexual partners.

According to the research organization The Heritage Foundation, it is disturbing to note that sexually active teenagers are "substantially less likely to be happy and more likely to be depressed" and "more likely to attempt suicide than are teenagers who are not sexually active."[2] The researchers noted that the sex education provided at schools is inadequate:

---

1. Robert E. Rector et al., "The Harmful Effects of Early Sexual Activity and Multiple Sexual Partners among Women: A Book of Charts," *The Heritage Foundation,* June 23, 2003, archived URL: http://bit.ly/EarlyHarm

2. Kirk A. Johnson, Lauren R. Noyes and Robert E. Rector, "Sexually Active Teenagers Are More Likely to Be Depressed and to Attempt Suicide," *The Heritage Foundation,* June 3, 2003, archived URL: http://bit.ly/DepressedTeens

"In general, these curricula fail to provide a strong message to delay sexual activity, fail to deal adequately with the long-term emotional and moral aspects of sexuality, and fail to provide students with the skills needed to develop intimate loving marital relationships as adults."

The researchers bring up a pertinent point. The sex education programs, like all other subjects taught at school, are designed to deliver information regarding sexual activity, including the risks, in a scientific, "value-neutral" way. However, at that young age, children need clear guidance from adults and possibly some rules and regulations, instead of being given clinical knowledge and then being left to make up their own minds about how and when to engage in sex, since they are not mature enough to handle, or even fully understand, the implications of their actions. Two principles prevalent in society today — that individuals have a right to make their own decisions and that indulging in sex is a pleasurable activity in which everyone should feel free to engage — create havoc when applied to immature youths.

Mirror, Mirror on the Wall...

Another effect of sexually permissive culture has been a heightened body consciousness, which pressurizes women to be constantly preoccupied with their looks and figure. The emphasis is more on outward appearance than on one's character, a value on which consumer culture thrives. A popular slogan in the advertising industry is 'sex sells,' and that's precisely what the media has been selling in rapidly increasing doses. As a result, when people in general conjure up an image of an attractive woman, they automatically think of movie actresses and supermodels who step out in the limelight dressed in designer clothes which no longer merely accentuate their curves, but blatantly expose them. The fact that Kim Kardashian – sometimes referred to as a glorified porn star since her claims to fame are a leaked sex-tape that she made with her boyfriend and the nude selfies that she regularly posts on the Internet – is today one of the most famous women on the planet, with more than a hundred million followers on Instagram, speaks volumes of the worth people attach to body image and their nonchalance when that image is publicly displayed.

In today's culture of media domination, the superstars created by the entertainment or fashion industries are not just some characters one views with mild amusement or interest, and dismisses while one gets on with the real business of life; they have been elevated to the level of role models. People want to look like them and live like them. Therefore, the scantily clad women are not adorning the billboards alone: they include the young girl wearing a tank top to college, the lady wearing spaghetti straps and shorts to go shopping, the executive wearing a tailored short skirt to the office, and the mother buying a backless prom dress for her daughter.

The cosmetic companies emerge as the clear beneficiaries of women's insecurities. Research shows that the average British woman spends up to £40,000 (an amount greater than a house deposit) in a lifetime on her hair and an astounding £100,000 on cosmetics.[1] The 2017 statistics report by American Society of Plastic Surgeons clearly shows that plastic surgery, a procedure

1. Lisa Sharkey, "Average British Woman Spends £140,000 on Hair and Cosmetics in Her Lifetime, Research Reveals," *Independent*, September 3, 2014, archived URL: http://bit.ly/ExpensiveHair

once considered the privilege of the rich and famous, has now become mainstream; 17.5 million cosmetic procedures, such as breast augmentation, liposuction, nose reshaping, and tummy tucks, were performed in the year 2017, amounting to a total cost of $16.7 billion.[1] These include 7.2 million procedures for removing wrinkles by injecting a toxin, popularly known as Botox, that temporarily paralyzes the muscles. Apart from the unnerving (pun intended) fact that Botox delivers a smooth face at the expense of losing control of certain facial muscles ("It's definitely a strange sensation as you go to lift your brows...but nothing moves.")[2] some psychologists fear that Botox treatments may be addictive, for its effect begins to wear off in four to six months, impelling women who have had the treatment once to go back for more.[3]

Society's preoccupation with appearances percolates to children as well. The popular kids at school are those who wear the trendiest clothes and shoes. Social media, with its trend of sharing pictures and videos, has added to the frenzy of wanting to always look one's best. Research conducted in the UK involving 1,000 children shows that they turn to consumer culture to fit in and make more friends, but in fact, it has the reverse effect and results in a negative, downward spiral for

---

1. ASPS National Clearinghouse of Plastic Surgery Procedural Statistics, "2017 Plastic Surgery Statistics Report," *American Society of Plastic Surgeons,* archived URL: http://bit.ly/PlasticStats
2. Samantha Freedman, "9 things I learnt from having botox in my 20s..." *Cosmopolitan,* October 29, 2018, archived URL: http://bit.ly/CosmoBotox
3. Lucy Rock, "Is America developing a 'crack-like addiction' to Botox beauty? How a culture hooked on body image is fuelling a dangerous trend," *The Guardian,* January 8, 2017, archived URL: http://bit.ly/BotoxAddict

them.[1] Affected by the perceived standard of attractiveness and thinness, even normal healthy girls begin to imagine themselves as obese and may become victims of eating disorders like anorexia (voluntary starvation) and bulimia (binge eating followed by forced purging), which in extreme cases can even lead to death.

No doubt the media is responsible for perpetuating unrealistic portrayals of beauty — an artificial façade created by cosmetics and clever camerawork, and more recently, by Photoshop — yet, our society is equally to blame to the extent it promotes the propaganda and encourages girls as young as five or six years old to wear strappy dresses, high heels and makeup. Children's beauty pageants have been popular for many decades in the US and have gradually been introduced in other parts of the world as well. Despite occasional protests, an American reality television series such as *Toddlers & Tiaras* (which aired from 2008 to 2013, and which followed the personal lives of families of contestants in child beauty pageants) had more than a million people tuning in every week to watch.

An article published by Fox News covering this issue quoted Annette Hill, the founder of Universal Royalty Child and Baby Beauty Pageants, who defends the pageants by stating that it makes the children "more assertive and vocal" and wants to know, "Besides, what is wrong with showing off your beautiful, talented daughter to the world?"[2] Rochelle Scott, the director

1. University of Sussex, "Pressure to be cool, look good is detrimental to many children," *ScienceDaily*, September 11, 2015, archived URL: http://bit.ly/CoolPressure

2. Hollie McKay, "Parents of Children on TLC's 'Toddlers in Tiaras' Hurting Their Kids, Critics Say," *Fox News*, last updated April 11, 2016, archived URL: http://bit.ly/TLChild

of California's Cover Miss and Cover Boy pageants, asserts, "Kids feel special when they have something sparkly on their head, even if it's not the winning tiara, it makes them feel good about themselves and the fact they accomplished something."

However, childhood behavioral health psychologist, Dr. Mike Bishop, debunks their claims: "Toddler beauty pageants set a superficial expectation about what makes someone beautiful — that beauty is primarily about your pose, your smile, your hair, and the clothes you wear. Self-worth should not be tied to competitions. Toddlers are not old enough to make an informed decision as to whether they should compete. Nor are they able to separate the competition from reality, which can make participation even more damaging to their self-esteem." In fact, he claims that these shows are popular precisely because "the damage done to beauty pageant toddlers' self-esteem often results in demanding and bratty behavior" which viewers find entertaining.

Psychologist Martina M. Cartwright points out other detrimental results for the young participants: "'The Princess Syndrome' as I like to call it, is a fairy tale. Unrealistic expectations to be thin, physically beautiful, and perfect are at the heart of some disordered eating behaviors and body dissatisfaction."[1] In addition, she says that in the process of being involved in these competitions, education of these young children suffers. "Long practice sessions are the norm and interfere with social activities, sleep and homework." The children are

---

1. Martina M. Cartwright, "Child Beauty Pageants: What Are We Teaching Our Girls? The princess syndrome, self-image and eating disorders," *Psychology Today*, August 12, 2011, archived URL: http://bit.ly/ChildPageants

under tremendous stress to perform and sadly, may harbor the belief that "parental and/or adult love or approval are anchored to how perfectly they look or how well they ignite the stage with their presence."

In 2005, alarmed by such media trends, the American Psychological Association (APA) established the Task Force on the Sexualization of Girls. The extensive research conducted by them details the far reaching consequences of sexual objectification of young girls.[1] They state that sexualization occurs when "a person's value comes only from his or her sexual appeal or behavior, to the exclusion of other characteristics." Their report provides ample evidence to show that the phenomenon is widespread by giving detailed description of its prevalence in television, music videos, music lyrics, movies, cartoons and animation, magazines, sports media, video games, Internet, advertising, products, clothing and cosmetics. For example, the Bratz dolls targeted for girls as young as four years olds are "marketed in bikinis, sitting in a hot tub, mixing drinks, and standing around." Clothing and retail stores are focusing on tweens (girls aged between seven and thirteen years) to sell "sexy lingerie" and other suggestive items that "once would have been marketed solely to adults." Five year old participants in child beauty pageants "wear fake teeth, hair extensions, and makeup and are encouraged to 'flirt' onstage by batting their long, false eyelashes." Disney's female characters "have more cleavage, fewer clothes, and are depicted as 'sexier' than those of yesteryear." In teen magazines girls and "young women are repeatedly encouraged to look and dress in specific

---

1. APA Task Force on the Sexualization of Girls, "Report of the APA Task Force on the Sexualization of Girls," *American Psychological Association,* 2007, archived URL: http://bit.ly/GirlReport

ways to look sexy for men, a phenomenon labeled 'costuming for seduction' and to use certain products in order to be more attractive to and desired by males."

Furthermore, the APA's Task Force study describes the negative effect of such sexualization on the girls' cognitive functioning, mental and physical health, relationships, attitudes and beliefs. It emphasizes that sexualization and objectification "undermine confidence in and comfort with one's own body, leading to a host of negative emotional consequences, such as shame, anxiety, and even self-disgust" and are linked to the three most common mental health problems — eating disorders, low self-esteem and depression.

The APA study points out that it is not only the girls who are affected, but, in fact the entire society is negatively impacted in many other ways. The boys are led to believe that the girls are simply to be treated as sex objects, and this deprives them from having respectful and healthy relationships with the opposite sex. The older ladies, seeing images of younger women dominate the media, are constantly fighting against time to stop the aging process. The sexualization and objectification of women also has more tragic consequences, such as sexual harassment and violence, which can scar the individuals — both the victim and the perpetrator — for life.

When ten-year-old Thylane Loubry Blondeau posed suggestively for *Vogue Paris (December 2010/January 2011 issue)* in a "provocative ensemble,"[1] the media may have expressed some concern regarding the fashion industry negatively

---

1. Vivian Giang, "This 10-Year-Old's Seductive Vogue Spread Is Making A Lot Of People Uncomfortable," *Business Insider*, August 5, 2011, archived URL: http://bit.ly/Age10

affecting "girls and women's images of themselves and their self-esteem"[1] and the fact that it inadvertently encourages "child predators." Journalists may have debated whether sixteen-year-old Miley Cyrus' pole-dancing performance at the 2009 Teen Choice Awards "sent the wrong message to her tween-age fans."[2] Yet reports such as the one painstakingly prepared by APA never hit mainstream media. In fact, articles that go into great detail about the 'shocking' clothes or behavior of these stars provide them with the much sought-after publicity they seek, as ironically controversial posts appear to be more popular than favorable ones. And thus, the industry — from clothing to accessories to cosmetics — immediately provides options for parents who allow, nay encourage, their children to mimic these celebrities.

Beauty Isn't Skin Deep

In the Vedic tradition too women were conscious about their physical appearance. The married ladies, in particular, would take great pains to make themselves attractive for their husbands. *Śrīmad-Bhāgavatam* describes that Kardama Muni, pleased by Devahūti's devotion towards him, manifested an aerial palace for her comfort. At that time he noticed her looking dissatisfied and could understand that she was concerned about her appearance because after years of austerity in the forest, her clothes were dirty and her hair was matted. So he at once arranged for a thousand maidservants to wait on her. Her elaborate beauty routine is described as follows:

1. Rheana Murray, "Thylane Loubry Blondeau photos: 10-year-old model's sultry Vogue spread sparks controversy," *Daily News*, August 4, 2012, archived URL: http://bit.ly/Model10

2. Monica Herrera, "Miley Cyrus' Pole Dance At Teen Choice Awards Sparks Controversy," *Billboard*, August 12, 2009, archived URL: http://bit.ly/TeenDance

> The girls, being very respectful to Devahūti, brought her forth, and after bathing her with valuable oils and ointments, they gave her fine, new, spotless cloth to cover her body. They then decorated her with very excellent and valuable jewels, which shone brightly. Next they offered her food containing all good qualities, and a sweet inebriating drink called *āsavam*. Then in a mirror she beheld her own reflection. Her body was completely freed from all dirt, and she was adorned with a garland. Dressed in unsullied robes and decorated with auspicious marks of *tilaka,* she was served very respectfully by the maids. Her entire body, including her head, was completely bathed, and she was decorated all over with ornaments. She wore a special necklace with a locket. There were bangles on her wrists and tinkling anklets of gold about her ankles. About her hips she wore a girdle of gold, set with numerous jewels, and she was further adorned with a precious pearl necklace and auspicious substances. Her countenance shone, with beautiful teeth and charming eyebrows. Her eyes, distinguished by lovely moist corners, defeated the beauty of lotus buds. Her face was surrounded by dark curling tresses.[1]

Of course, Kardama Muni was a great sage and his wife a princess, but in Vedic culture, even ordinary women would decorate themselves with gold jewelry. They would use natural cosmetics such as kohl to darken their eyes and oils to keep the skin glowing and fragrant. They would take pride in maintaining long, luxuriant hair. Śrīla Prabhupāda comments that their purpose in bedecking themselves was not to satisfy their own vanity, but to inspire their husbands:

---

1. *Śrīmad-Bhāgavatam* 3.23.28–33.

> A woman is generally accustomed to dress herself nicely with fine garments and decorative ornaments. She may even sometimes wear flowers in her hair. Women especially dress themselves up in the evening because the husband comes home in the evening after working hard all day. It is the duty of the wife to dress herself up very nicely so that when her husband returns home he becomes attracted by her dress and cleanliness and thus becomes satisfied. In other words, the wife is the inspiration of all good intelligence.[1]

The same lady would dress plainly when her husband was not around.

> According to Yājñavalkya's religious injunctions, a woman whose husband is away from home should not take part in any social functions, should not decorate her body, should not laugh and should not go to any relative's house in any circumstance. This is the vow of the ladies whose husbands are away from home. At the same time, it is also enjoined that a wife should never present herself before the husband in an unclean state. She must decorate herself with ornaments and good dress and should always be present before the husband in a happy and joyous mood.[2]

In this way, the married women would dress themselves up exquisitely to keep their husbands satisfied. But, at the same time, Vedic culture revolves around the spirit of renunciation. People in general were taught not to be attached to their youthful beauty nor to try to reverse the aging process, despite the fact that in those days they were familiar with the science

1. *Śrīmad-Bhāgavatam* 4.27.2, purport by Śrīla Prabhupāda.
2. *Śrīmad-Bhāgavatam* 1.11.31, purport by Śrīla Prabhupāda.

of restoring and preserving youth in a much more sophisticated manner than the plastic surgery options available today. For example, Cyavana Muni took the help of the Aśvinī-kumāra brothers, the heavenly physicians, to transform his old and shriveled up body into that of "a very beautiful young man, as bright as the sun."[1] As the citizens would advance in years, they were expected to devote more and more time for spiritual life. After the *gṛhastha-āśrama,* or married life, the couple would enter into *vānaprastha-āśrama,* or leading a retired life, which involved living in the forest and visiting places of pilgrimage. Śrīla Prabhupāda explains:

> The *vānaprastha* stage is exactly like this. Although the wife remains with the husband, she undergoes severe austerities and penances so that although both husband and wife live together, there is no question of sex. [...] The wife is expected to give up all luxurious habits. She should not even dress nicely or comb her hair. Hair-combing is one of the main businesses of women. In the *vānaprastha* stage the wife should not take care of her hair. Thus her hair will become tangled in knots. Consequently, the wife will no longer be attractive to the husband, and she herself will no longer be agitated by sex impulses. In this way both husband and wife can advance in spiritual consciousness. This advanced stage is called the *paramahaṁsa* stage, and once it is obtained, both husband and wife can be actually liberated from bodily consciousness.[2]

The Vedic idea of beauty was not limited to the natural charm of youth or having the perfect hourglass figure. Śrīla Prabhupāda mentions:

1. *Śrīmad-Bhāgavatam* 9.3.11-18.
2. *Śrīmad-Bhāgavatam* 4.28.44, purport by Śrīla Prabhupāda.

> Generally a woman becomes more beautiful when, after an early marriage, she gives birth to a child. To give birth to a child is the natural function of a woman, and therefore a woman becomes more and more beautiful as she gives birth to one child after another.[1]

Although the women maintained themselves for the pleasure of their husbands, they were not panic-stricken at the sight of white hair or wrinkles. The main reason was that Vedic culture teaches one to appreciate qualities such as kindness, devotion, and simplicity far more than an attractive face or a shapely figure. Also, one is encouraged to face the reality of passing time and understand the transient nature of the material world. Thus, the ladies were secure in the knowledge that their husbands would not abandon them on account of their fleeting good looks.

As far as young, unmarried girls were concerned, there was no need for them to dress in a provocative manner in order to attract the attention of young men. Their parents, looking out for them, would make arrangements to get them married to suitable men, similar to them in temperament. The Vedic culture was fiercely protective of the women and children and there was no question of "showing off [one's] beautiful, talented daughter to the world." The girls would often receive instruction on *catuḥ-ṣaṣṭi-kalās,* or 64 different forms of art, which included several years of systematic training in classical music, dance and drama, but they would perform only for the pleasure of their deities at home, or in front of a select audience of close family members.

---

1. *Śrīmad-Bhāgavatam* 4.24.12, purport by Śrīla Prabhupāda.

The Vedic system allowed the girls to have a carefree childhood, the ladies to indulge in the feminine desire to dress up, keep house and have children while they were married, and the elderly women to enjoy a position of respect in the society and the freedom to pursue spiritual life.

Inviting Modesty

I remember feeling great indignation and fury at the unwanted advances of strangers in my youth — the stares, the vulgar remarks, the surreptitious groping — it was all quite horrible and I fervently wished that the men would be better behaved and would just leave us women alone. My friends and I grumbled and fretted, and blamed them for presuming that if a girl is wearing a revealing outfit she is willing to go out with any man who approaches her. We shrugged off advice coming from 'prudes' who disapproved of our clothes or the fact that we chose to stay out late. We reasoned that some men are just lecherous — it doesn't matter what we wear, they eye every girl with lust. And anyway, "rape happens because of the rapist" and has nothing to do with the victim's behavior or dress, right?

Fast forward a few years, my fascination for traditional culture made me exchange my figure-hugging pants and short skirts for sarees and, much to the chagrin of my peers, I even began to cover my hair when I went out. That's when I really began to realize the truth of the statement that the onus lies on both the sides. Now, the same men who would be lounging around 'checking out' girls passing by, would respectfully stand aside to let me pass. While waiting in lines at the airport or check-out counters of supermarkets, men would not engage in frivolous conversation while trying to gauge whether I too was 'interested.' Gone were the indecent stares and suggestive remarks! It was as though carrying myself with dignity provided an invisible shield around me.

This may sound almost dismal to young girls who are in fact interested in attracting some attention from the opposite sex. But if one considers how often we get that attention from the wrong kind of men, it would be worth our while to consider whether we want to risk it. I realized that, in today's world, if we style our hair and wear clothes and make-up to specifically attract men's attention, it is unrealistic to expect that we will be able to pick and choose which men should be attracted.

I started to see that there was a wide range of men between the perfect gentleman and the die-hard lecher or the criminal rapist. These are men who, confused by the media's portrayal of women, want to take advantage of women and enjoy if possible, but they are also capable of behaving respectfully when they see a cultured woman. Our conduct may not make a difference to the pathologically sick rapist, but it makes a world of difference in the normal world when we are among normal men, which is most of the time.

Dressing decently and behaving modestly may not make us very popular,[1] but it will preserve our self-respect and eventually help us to face the world with a new confidence.

My elder daughter is now fifteen years old. She has had very limited interaction with boys; she has never had a friend who

---

1. In the preface of the 15th edition of her book *A Return to Modesty: Discovering the Lost Virtue,* Wendy Shalit describes the animosity she faced in her college because of her perceived "prudish ways:" "Students who were perfect strangers would give me the finger, and when I arrived at my apartment, I would often receive anonymous, nasty e-mails addressed to 'you overdressed little you.'"

is a boy, let alone a boyfriend. Yet, she doesn't feel like she's missing something in life. Naturally she is intrigued with the idea of being in a relationship with a boy, but is willing to wait till she meets the one she is going to marry, to experience it. In the meantime, she is content to spend time with her family and forge strong relationships with the girls who are her 'besties.'[1] Unencumbered by things like 'going steady' and 'breaking up' she has experienced none of the anxiety and insecurities that are normally associated with teenagers today. As a result, not only is she able to approach academics with a focused mind (she is the youngest in her school to be appearing for the high school certificate examination), she has enough time and mental bandwidth to learn musical instruments, classical dance, and art. I'm glad that her growing up years are filled with 'good, clean fun' instead of incidents that would make her cringe with regret when she looks back at them.

Just Don't Do It

The famous Nike slogan 'Just Do It', although primarily aimed to enthuse people to exercise — while wearing Nike gear — also symbolizes the casual attitude of the current age, of 'just doing' something without giving it serious thought beforehand. But, as noted above, this is hardly a sensible approach, particularly in the context of physical relations between men and women. Women, despite their bravado, are sad and disappointed at the end of day, when physical intimacy doesn't culminate in a meaningful relationship. Even if they eventually end up with their true love, that relationship is likely to be marred by the fallout from previous unsuccessful relationships, for each heartbreak leaves a woman somewhat more cynical and defensive.

1. Teenager slang for best friends.

Until a few decades ago, there was a clear distinction in society between respectable women and prostitutes — in the way they behaved and dressed, and subsequently were treated. But as men became less than ideal, most women activists claimed that women alone should not be expected to uphold high moral standards, and so they brought about a culture where the distinction between the two classes of women largely blurred. Yet, even while women relinquished their own responsibility of following the code of conduct of respectable women, they demanded the right to be treated like one. This attitude is perfectly demonstrated at the SlutWalks where women protest against rape culture while "strutting [their] stuff."[1] At these events, women deliberately dress as prostitutes to emphasize that their appearance should not be used as an excuse for rape.

Unfortunately, one can't have one's cake and eat it too. If a woman dresses inappropriately, it certainly does not mean that she is 'asking for it' and deserves to be violated, but it cannot be denied that in doing so, she is willingly participating in a culture that promotes sensual pleasure and body consciousness.. They are not wrong in their expectation that men should behave like gentlemen, but how reasonable is that demand when it's coming from women who refuse to behave like ladies? Although this proposal might still have worked in the bygone days when men were truly virtuous,[2] in the current age, having

1. About The Walk. Take the power away from derogatory labels, *Amber Rose SlutWalk,* archived URL: http://bit.ly/SlutMarch

2. The *Mahābhārata* relates the incident of prince Arjuna rejecting the sexual advances of the eternally youthful celestial angel, Urvaśī. He explained that he considered her to be his mother, since thousands of years ago she was the wife of one of his ancestors, King Purūravā. Despite Urvaśī's persuasive arguments that the human moral code was not applicable in the heavenly planets, Arjuna remained undeterred.

stricter laws or organizing more protest marches championing individual freedom is unlikely to bring about a substantial change. The only hope for men and women to honor and respect each other is to work towards genuinely uplifting the moral standards of the entire society, which begins with women behaving modestly and men being self-controlled.

The sexual revolution and the feminist movement have worked hand-in-hand to allow women to behave and dress as daringly as they please without being censored. This is celebrated as women's freedom of choice. However, the consequences for women, in the long run, have been that in exchange for some frivolous sensual pleasure, they have lost their respectability and ended up in a far more vulnerable position. Particularly poignant is the fact that at the present moment, issues related to sexual behavior and body image are not just impacting grown women, but are increasingly affecting young girls as well.

For youngsters, the desire to fit in is so strong that it may be very difficult for them to go against the flow. But they must be encouraged to consider that what they do with their bodies is certainly going to affect their minds, and that those impressions will remain for a long time. Due to peer pressure, a young girl may be reluctant to refuse a date with a cool guy despite knowing that his intentions are not noble; she may be unwilling to stay in the dorm instead of attending a hip party that will involve alcohol and drugs; she may be unsure about dressing decently when the trend dictates otherwise; but if she understands that her self-worth does not have to be defined by the opinions of the popular kids, then she will get the willpower to live her life on her own terms, in a civilized, cultured way.

Ideally, young girls should be taught to value their chastity. In addition, they should be given such a loving environment at home that they never have to turn to shallow flings to gain some affection or attention. Society finally needs to call the media bluff — sexual pleasure doesn't equate with happiness. This, then, would be the real empowerment for the women — when we empower them to say 'No' to being exploited in the name of liberalization.

Vedic Culture for Modern Women

Several aspects of Vedic culture can be seen in other traditional cultures throughout the world. Even in the Western world, a few generations ago, women were protected by their families and would go out only in the company of a chaperone. They were homeschooled and their marriages were arranged. Their primary role was that of a homemaker. However, at one point in modernity, the above arrangements were perceived as mistreatment and subjugation of women. Subsequently, as a result of protests led by women activists, the social fabric in the West changed drastically, and the rest of the world followed suit.

We are grateful to the women's movement for bringing women's issues to the forefront, for there is no doubt that the problems are real. But their proposed solutions, combined with rapidly deteriorating moral standards, have created bigger problems. Feminists experimented with creating a new world order in which every individual, man, woman, and even a child, has to look after themselves. Countering misogyny with misandry has led to deep distrust between men and women, and caused the breakdown of the family unit.

It's as though the women, being disappointed with the men, sought to prove that they can be just as bad!

Perhaps the world would be a different place if they had urged society as a whole to live up to the ideals given in the religious scriptures. Perhaps the reformation that was needed was to encourage the men to genuinely follow their duties and the women to sincerely follow theirs, rather than inventing a new set of duties which are not in harmony with their physical and mental characteristics.

Tranquil Within

At the present moment, women are under immense stress, being tugged in one direction by their own desire to marry and have children, and in another to fulfill the overwhelming expectation to carve out a successful career. A large section of women activists tried to do away with marriage and childbearing altogether, so that they would be free to pursue their own interests. But since these two life stages are a source of great satisfaction for women, what has essentially happened is that they are left chasing the elusive work-life balance and getting exhausted in the bargain. The state of the housewives is no better, for they are made to feel useless since they do not bring home a pay packet every month.

The traditional model is being offered as an alternative because, when practiced properly, it allows a woman to be peaceful for she has the freedom to indulge her feminine side while remaining in the shelter of a loving family. The proposal is not that women simply lounge around at home while the men go to work, nor even that they spend the entire day mechanically engaged in household chores — that would eventually lead to frustration and a sense of emptiness. But a woman who fills her day with meaningful activities, while looking after the physical, emotional and spiritual needs of her family, will be content and will feel fulfilled.

In today's competitive world, following traditional gender roles may not facilitate the most luxurious standard of living, but it helps in creating a harmonious family life, which in turn provides a conducive environment for devotional life. It allows a woman to be fruitfully engaged according to her nature, while remaining tranquil within.

Such a traditional woman is neither lazy nor irresponsible. She is not a passive weakling who can be pushed around. Her calm demeanor belies an inner strength that comes from abiding by the word of God. She has no need to canvass for her rights because her actions command a respect that no laws could ever grant. Her determination to do the right thing uplifts not just her own, but also the consciousness of all those around her.

I admit that there are exceptions to the rule: women who are genuinely not maternal by nature and are therefore not at their peaceful best within a family, or a husband and wife who are able to manage just fine with the roles reversed, i.e. the woman being the head of the family, while the husband is content to remain in the background. But clearly, these are exceptions and not the desired ideal as the feminists would have us believe. The attempt of the past few decades to obliterate the inherent tendencies of men and women has created a society full of conflict. Therefore, this presentation has been centered around principles which hold true for the majority, for at this stage, it is imperative that we re-establish the general rule, rather than focus on catering to the exceptions.

The Way Forward: Revival and Reconciliation

In a discussion of a revival of traditional culture, several questions crop up. The modern culture may have its shortcomings, but traditional culture is almost obsolete, so even if one is able to appreciate the principles of ancient culture, how is it going to work? Who is going to do it? Where does one begin? How does one practically apply these principles in one's life?

Culture needs a framework of society around it. A woman cannot perform her duties in isolation, particularly in a traditional set-up. For her to adopt a more submissive role, it is essential that she is surrounded by people who are willing to protect and appreciate her, and not abuse her humility. So the change that will be required is not just in the attitude or actions of women, but society itself will have to change its outlook for any real change to be effective. Although our discussion is centered on women's roles, clearly this is just one part of a complicated jigsaw puzzle, and a full-fledged revival can take place only when the other pieces fall into place. The traditional woman requires the wise elders, the noble husband and the supportive community members in order to properly manifest.

So then, who is going to do it? May I suggest that it should be a collective effort, in which both men and women resolve to cooperate. But at the present moment, the men complain that they cannot demonstrate their good intentions to protect the women unless the women change their attitudes and become less cynical and defensive. On the other hand, the women claim that they are reluctant to accept a more submissive role for fear of being taken for granted and being neglected.

And yet, someone has to take the first step. If men and women keep passing the buck, we are likely to remain in a vicious cycle in which the consciousness of both rapidly spirals downwards. The past century has witnessed the power of women's voices. They have struggled to bring about tremendous cultural changes. However, the dynamics of society keep changing and a thoughtful activist should change her stand accordingly. If convinced, women can now be instrumental in initiating a revival of traditional culture. They are ingenious enough to reconcile it with the current culture. Without doubt if they set their heart on it, they will be able to garner support from all factions of society.

Śrīla Prabhupāda has explained that in one sense women are more powerful than men because by their sweet temperament they inspire the men to be better:

> As far as the women class are concerned, they are accepted as a power of inspiration for men. As such, women are more powerful than men. Mighty Julius Caesar was controlled by a Cleopatra.[1]

The cause of traditional culture will be furthered greatly if women resolutely get behind it. At the same time, it cannot be

1. *Śrīmad-Bhāgavatam* 1.9.27, purport by Śrīla Prabhupāda.

emphasized enough that a change of attitude will be required on the part of *both* men and women.

But, where does one begin? One begins on an individual level, in our circle of influence. Often, that is how changes are brought about; they begin small and then gain momentum. A mother teaches these values to her children while adopting them herself. She inspires her friends, she discusses them with her family, and so it goes on.

And finally, how does one practically apply these principles in one's life? This, of course, is the most crucial question and requires careful consideration. The application will depend on individuals and their unique situations. For example, it may not be possible for a twenty-first-century American woman to follow the principle of submitting to an arranged marriage, and she may have no choice but to date men if she hopes to meet her future husband, but she can certainly conduct herself in a dignified manner during such encounters, in keeping with principles of shyness and chastity.

In other situations, a woman may have no male member to protect her and may have to have an outside job to support herself and her family. Such a lady can follow traditional culture by dressing conservatively, and keeping her interaction with the men at work strictly professional. She may also consider job options which allows her to remain in the company of women and children, or to work from home.

Irrespective of one's background or faith, women can resolve to be loving mothers and respectful wives, to become pillars of support for their families. Today's internet-savvy, educated mothers can view routine jobs at home, such as cooking and organizing, as challenging mini-projects. If there's a need for them to contribute to the family income, they can consider options such as working as freelancers or running internet-based businesses, which will give them the flexibility to work in a way that they do not have to compromise their responsibilities at home.

Words of Caution

While talking about practically making traditional gender roles work in our lives, it is important to remember that the most significant aspect of traditional culture is that it has God in the center. It is neither easy for a woman to be submissive nor for a man to work hard to provide for his family, but when they perform their duties with an aim to help one another come to a higher level of consciousness, they will be willing to sacrifice and practice humility. They are naturally kind and respectful, because their minds are not preoccupied with trying to enjoy life to the maximum. The culture is hinged on its individuals being noble-minded and having a higher goal in life. Without this understanding, it is inevitable that those in authority will exploit their subordinates, and women will be left disillusioned and bitter. Thus, those who are serious about following traditional culture should be even more serious about their spiritual lives.

Another important consideration is that culture is a complex entity, which cannot be fully understood by theoretical discussions. Those who are serious about adopting traditional culture should not only familiarize themselves with the principles, but should also spend enough time studying communities which are practicing such culture successfully.

Otherwise, there are many subtle nuances that one may miss completely. For example, a person may think that in the patriarchal family, the man alone is the decision maker and the woman has to accept his word without a murmur. In actuality, the woman is an equal partner (hence called *ardhāṅginī*, or better half) and is allowed to voice her opinion. The only difference is that the etiquette demands that she submits her view respectfully, and in case of a difference of opinion gracefully concedes. Also, between husband and wife there is a tacit understanding about who handles which sphere, and they have the freedom to take decisions in that area.

Even the most well-meaning attempts at reviving Vedic culture will fail if we lose sight of the spiritual goal or if the principles are implemented piecemeal. Historically, these are the two main reasons for rejection of traditional culture, and we should be careful to avoid them. Just as deviation from principles creates havoc in society, so does fanatical application.

Why Not Start a Revolution?

Even adopting just a few aspects of the culture properly can make a radical difference in our lives. However, it will be truly effective only when all the elements are working in synergy with each other. For many of us, it would require a complete paradigm shift. But at the same time, it is not impossible. Many generations have lived by the codes of this culture in the past, and many continue to do so even in the present times, and even in Western countries. One who is determined should seek the right people for guidance and support. In today's interconnected world, new concepts and lifestyles can be explored in depth with the help of the Internet.

This discussion is especially relevant for the next generation. We need to show them both sides of the coin before allowing them to decide how they want to shape their lives. We should be honest enough to analyze whether our life choices have delivered the result we expected them to, and if not, then we must consider how things may be done differently. After years of believing in a certain value system, it is hard to sit back and objectively question it, but we owe it to ourselves and our children to be willing to bring back traditions that in the past have helped create happy families and stable societies.

In particular, countries in which traditional culture still dominates should make efforts to preserve it. Even as they are rapidly adopting Western culture, Indians are complacent because they think that they can have the best of both the worlds — they can indulge in sophisticated sensual pleasures and the safety net of their culture will prevent them from going too far. However, culture is not picked up by osmosis alone, just by being in an environment where individuals are practicing it to varying degrees. Important aspects need to be discussed and explained, especially in the current age where everyone has a challenging attitude and the tendency is to view anything traditional as unscientific, sentimental, and essentially worthless. Individuals who have experienced the joy of being in a conflict-free environment while growing up amidst a large, loving family ought to give credit to their culture where it is due, and make a conscious attempt to be instrumental in continuing the legacy.

While ancient culture has been vilified as primitive and repressive, in actuality it is based on principles that help create a balanced society in which men and women complement, rather than compete with, each other. The principles of traditional culture are as relevant to women today as they were hundreds of years ago, although naturally the application will differ according to time, place and circumstance. In fact, I would contend that Vedic culture is more relevant today than ever before, for it's the only hope we have of bringing some semblance of serenity into the lives of individuals who are currently harassed due to inner conflict, domestic strife, and work-related stress.

It is time for women to reverse the direction of change into one that actually favors them. It would require courage and sacrifice, for it is never easy to go against predominant trends, but it behooves them to consider what truly gives them satisfaction and examine whether modern culture is helping them to achieve that.

It is time for women to reclaim tranquility into their lives.

Women are inherently powerful. They do not need 50% of the seats reserved for them in parliament or on the board of directors of corporates to realize that. Their strength lies not in replacing the men in their domain, but instead in performing their duty in such an exemplary manner that the men are inspired to follow their own. Making it on the list of the richest people in the world is not the only way to achieve prestige and respect. If women adhere to high moral standards, they are in a position to demand the same of the rest of the society and are capable of completely transforming the current state of the world.

Why not start a revolution?

Real Success: Health, Wealth and Happiness

For me the revolution began the day I started to marvel at the undefeatable logic of Vedic philosophy.

The world that I grew up in taught me that success in life essentially meant having an enviable career. I believed that a job would provide two important things — the means to attain material comfort and security, and the intellectual satisfaction of working out solutions to complicated problems.

However, the scriptures revealed an altogether different definition of success. The *Vedas* emphasize that life is meant for a higher purpose than making money to achieve material comfort. Of course, one's basic needs have to be met, but for that it is not necessary for every member of the family aged between eighteen and eighty to be out working from nine to five. As for intellectual stimulation, real satisfaction would be derived from attempting to resolve the truly complex problems of life — who we are, why we are here and what the real goal of human existence is. I was fascinated to discover that each verse in the scriptures had a profound meaning, infinitely more complex than the most complex computer algorithm I had ever studied or worked with, and yet, at the same time was directly relevant to me. I began to realize that there was a whole dimension to my existence that I was previously unaware of, and that my true worth need not be measured by what rung of the corporate ladder I am on. That is when I started to explore an alternative way of life.

Practically speaking, it was a process of trial and error. I accepted the role of a housewife but I did not know how to cook or clean. I wanted to be a submissive and dutiful daughter-in-law and wife, but was woefully lacking in self-control. However, my strong faith in the scriptures gave me the determination to continue to endeavor. I approached ladies, such as my mother-in-law, who were adept in household tasks and asked them to take me under their wing. I took advice from my grandmother about behaving appropriately with other family members, accommodating unexpected guests and being meticulous about details around the house. I spoke with women who had had a traditional upbringing to learn the subtleties of gentle behavior.

I turned to the Internet for stain-removal tips, for arts and crafts projects to keep my children engaged, and for recipes that I spent many hours experimenting and perfecting. I joined a support group of ladies who were committed to following the word of the scriptures and who understood that traditional culture was an essential part of the spiritual equation. These were women from different parts of the world and I was encouraged by their enthusiasm and earnestness. I followed the blogs of ladies who were inspired to follow a more natural and simple lifestyle and read about how they handled the challenges I was facing. I derived inspiration from historical narrations of women mentioned in the *Vedas* and aspired to follow their example.

It wasn't easy for me to go against the conditioning I had undergone for most of my life but almost immediately I could perceive the positive change in my life.

As I started on my spiritual journey, accepting the role recommended for a woman, the first thing that I noticed was that I was healthier, both in body and in mind. My backache vanished and the throat infections dropped in their frequency from monthly to annual. Being home was not only conducive to my own physical well-being, but it also allowed my family to flourish by having home-cooked food tailored to their individual needs. In addition, having a wholesome, vegetarian diet and a regulated lifestyle proved to be beneficial.

The next surprising result of following Vedic culture was the prosperity that came our way. By accepting the Vedic principle that one should be satisfied with one's lot, even though we were living on a single income, we always felt that we had more than enough. We did not cut corners, but at the same time we did not spend our earnings frivolously. In Vedic culture, a householder is liberal in sharing whatever he has with others. Accordingly, we often invited guests home, and also contributed a portion of our earnings for worthy causes. We realized that real wealth has little to do with one's bank balance; real wealth is to have a generous heart. As it happened, by God's grace, my husband did very well in his career. Within a short span of time, he was on the board of multi-billion dollar companies and the financial advisor to some of the wealthiest men in the world. And yet, we were careful not to get attached to living an opulent lifestyle. At the age of thirty-five, having saved and invested wisely, my husband chose to walk away from his career to engage in full-time voluntary service.

But the most precious gift that I received from following traditional, Vedic culture was having my days pervaded with a deep sense of peace and happiness. This was unlike anything I had previously experienced and came from the contentment of following my duties to please the Lord of the universe.

Being a daughter, wife and mother was naturally joyous, but performing these roles became deeply fulfilling for me when God was kept in the center. Achieving health and wealth were unexpected side-effects, and I acknowledge that while they are here today, they may be gone tomorrow, but the tranquility in my life is not dependent on external factors and I know that it will remain with me so long as I remain in the shelter of scriptural injunctions.

I am far from perfect in my role as a devotee, wife, or mother, but when I look back at my life, I feel satisfied that I have spent my time trying my best to serve the Supreme Lord, follow His instructions regarding my duty, and share His message with others. I have a purpose in life, a loving family and peace in my heart. This, then, is my real success. And it can be yours, if you sincerely follow a God-centered culture — be it Vedic tradition, Christianity, Islam, Judaism or any other that inspires you to lead a life that is physically, mentally, and spiritually fulfilling.

I invite you, dear reader, to give careful thought to things that really make you happy, and I encourage you to tread a path less traveled if it helps you reach a place of joy and serenity.

Epilogue

Dear Cousin,

I choose not to work because I find my job as a wife and mother to be more rewarding than anything that the corporate or research world can ever offer.

I choose not to call my husband by his first name because in Vedic culture we don't do so out of respect for elders — just as you call my elder sister 'Didi' instead of using her first name, because she's older than you. I am courteous to my husband because I am grateful for all that he does for our family. I'm grateful that he went to work, day after day, year after year, tolerating unreasonable bosses and conniving co-workers, long commutes, and demanding travels to ensure that his family has all the comforts. I'm grateful that he spent months being both mother and father to my elder daughter when I was completely preoccupied with the birth of the younger one. I'm grateful that when I had a slipped disc he would come back from work and immediately enter the kitchen, and he and the girls would cook up innovative meals. I'm grateful that he encourages me to pray, teach, and write.

I choose to live in Mayapur because I want to be among people who are philosophical and thoughtful. I also choose to live here because it is green and peaceful, and I want my children to romp around, be carefree, and play like we did when we were young. I want them to live without being overwhelmed by the trappings of a big city. I choose to send them to the school here because along with academics, they are also encouraged to ponder about deeper questions of life.

I choose to give them fresh fruits, preferably organic, because – well, it's healthy! The improvement in their health since they've started having produce from our garden and the local farms is clearly visible.

Please don't be concerned on my account. My life is simple, but sweet. I have spent a long time processing my choices, and I'm at peace with them. In fact, I wouldn't want to change a single thing.

Why don't you join me?

Lots of love,

Indira.

Acknowledgements

I am eternally grateful to Śrīla Prabhupāda, the greatest ambassador of Vedic culture. His teachings have transformed my life.

This book owes its existence to my spiritual guide, His Holiness Bhakti Vikāsa Swami. Inspired by a seminar delivered by him on women's role in Vedic culture, I began to write on this subject, initially in the form of an essay. His confidence in me persuaded me to start working on this book. I am indebted to him for his encouragement and for his generous offer that I could freely take material from his published works.

I am thankful to my family for adjusting their lives so that I had enough time to write. My husband, Tapana Miśra Dāsa, has been my pillar of support. His patience in handling all the nitty-gritties, despite his own busy schedule, helped see this project to fruition in record time. The enthusiasm of my dear daughers, Krishangi and Gaurangi kept me buoyed up.

A special thanks to Advaita Candra Prabhu, of Torchlight Publishing, for his support, suggestions, and advice. My deepest thanks to Phalini Devi Dasi, Nārada Priyā Devī Dāsī, Sundarī Rādhikā Devī Dāsī, and Mālyahāri-kuṇḍa Dāsī for their kind words and loyal support. Their determination to adopt a culture they were not born in, has been a source of inspiration. I would like to express my appreciation for Gaurāṅgī Gāndharvikā Devī Dāsī, Govinda-priyā Devī Dāsī, Vipanchi, and all the other reviewers for their pertinent feedback on the original manuscript. I am thankful to Dāru Brahman Prabhu for his words of encouragement and his kind offer to do the final proofreading.

I am greatly indebted to the production team at Bhakti Vikas Trust for working tirelessly to transform the manuscript into a book. I would also like to extend my gratitude towards the team of proofreaders who meticulously went through the manuscript and gave valuable suggestions to refine it: Rāma Kumāra Dāsa, Narottama Priya Dāsa, Lalitā Sakhī Devī Dāsī, Nārāyana Padmanābha Dāsa, Ananta Sarovara Devī Dāsī, Lavaṅga Devī Dāsī, Jāmbavān Dāsa, Śraddha Dāsī, and Helen Scott.

My editor, Dhīra Lalitā Devī Dāsī, has done more than just iron out the rough spots, which were innumerous in themselves. I am grateful not only for her professional abilities, but also for the fact that we are on the same page. I'm happy to have had her by my side on this (in her words) 'transcendental adventure'.

About the Author

Indira Meshram, a computer engineer by profession and housewife by choice, has been on both sides of the fence. An alumni of the Indian Institute of Technology, she holds a master's degree in Computer Science, and her research has been published in international academic journals. She worked for large corporations before deciding to quit her full-time job to pursue her dream of achieving true fulfillment. An avid traveler, she has visited more than forty countries, which helped her gain an appreciation for both Western and Oriental cultures. She is an initiated member of the International Society for Krishna Consciousness. She lives with her husband and two daughters in a community founded on the principle of 'simple living and high thinking,' and spends her time teaching, writing, and baking.

His Divine Grace A.C. Bhaktivedanta Swami Prabhupāda

Founder-*Ācārya* of the International Society for Krishna Consciousness

About Śrīla Prabhupāda

His Divine Grace A.C. Bhaktivedanta Swami Prabhupāda appeared in this world in 1896 in Calcutta (now Kolkata).

In 1922, after completing college, he first met his guru, Śrīla Bhaktisiddhānta Sarasvatī Ṭhākura — a prominent religious scholar and the founder of the Gauḍīya Maṭha spiritual institution — who entreated him to dedicate his life to broadcasting Vedic knowledge in the English language. Śrīla Prabhupāda became his follower and, in 1933, was formally initiated as his disciple.

In the following years, Śrīla Prabhupāda wrote a commentary on the *Bhagavad-gītā,* rendered assistance to the Gauḍīya Maṭha, and in 1944 started *Back to Godhead,* an English fortnightly magazine. Single-handedly, he edited it, typed the manuscripts, checked the galley proofs, and even distributed the individual copies. Today, *Back to Godhead* is being continued by his followers.

In 1950, Śrīla Prabhupāda retired from married life to devote more time to study, writing, and preaching. For that purpose, he travelled to the holy city of Vṛndāvana, where he lived in humble circumstances in the historic temple of Rādhā-Dāmodara.

In 1959, Śrīla Prabhupāda accepted *sannyāsa* (formal renunciation of family life for full dedication to spiritual pursuits). At Rādhā-Dāmodara, he began work on a multivolume commentated translation of the eighteen-thousand-verse *Śrīmad-Bhāgavatam*. He also wrote *Easy Journey to Other Planets*.

In August 1965, after publishing three volumes of the *Bhāgavatam*, Śrīla Prabhupāda set out to the United States to fulfil the mission of his guru. When he first arrived, by freighter, he was practically penniless. After almost a year of great difficulty, in July of 1966 he established the International Society for Krishna Consciousness.

Before his passing away, on 14 November 1977, Śrīla Prabhupāda had guided the Society and seen it grow to a worldwide confederation of more than one hundred ashrams, schools, temples, institutes, and farm communities. He had also inspired the construction of several major temples in India, including the international headquarters of ISKCON, at Māyāpur, West Bengal, the site of a developing Vedic city. In Vṛndāvana, Uttar Pradesh, is the magnificent Kṛṣṇa-Balarāma Temple. ISKCON also has established several other major temples throughout the world.

Yet Śrīla Prabhupāda's most significant contribution was his books. He wrote more than fifty volumes of authoritative commentated translations and summary studies of the philosophical and religious classics of India. Highly respected by scholars for their authority, depth, and clarity, over five hundred million copies have been printed in more than eighty languages. The Bhaktivedanta Book Trust, established in 1972 to publish the works of His Divine Grace A. C. Bhaktivedanta Swami Prabhupāda, has thus become the world's largest publisher of books in the field of Indian religion and philosophy.

Despite his advanced age, Śrīla Prabhupāda circled the globe fourteen times in just twelve years, on lecture tours that brought him to six continents. And amidst such a rigorous schedule, he continued to write prolifically. Indeed, Śrīla Prabhupāda's writings constitute a veritable library of Vedic philosophy, religion, literature, and culture.

Books by Śrīla Prabhupāda

Bhagavad-gītā As It Is

Śrīmad-Bhāgavatam (18 vols.; with disciples)

Śrī Caitanya-caritāmṛta (9 vols.)

Kṛṣṇa, The Supreme Personality of Godhead

Teachings of Lord Caitanya

The Nectar of Devotion

The Nectar of Instruction

Śrī Īśopaniṣad

Light of the Bhāgavata

Easy Journey to Other Planets

The Science of Self Realization

Kṛṣṇa Consciousness: The Topmost Yoga System

Perfect Questions, Perfect Answers

Teachings of Lord Kapila, the Son of Devahūti

Transcendental Teachings of Prahlāda Mahārāja

Teachings of Queen Kuntī

Kṛṣṇa, the Reservoir of Pleasure

The Path of Perfection

Life Comes from Life

Message of Godhead

The Perfection of Yoga

Beyond Birth and Death

On the Way to Kṛṣṇa

Rāja-Vidyā: The King of Knowledge

Elevation to Kṛṣṇa Consciousness

Kṛṣṇa Consciousness: The Matchless Gift

Nārada-bhakti-sūtra (with disciples)

Mukunda-mālā-stotra (with disciples)

A Second Chance

The Journey of Self-Discovery

The Laws of Nature: An Infallible Justice

Renunciation Through Wisdom

Civilization and Transcendence

The Quest for Enlightenment

Dharma: The Way of Transcendence

Introduction to Bhagavad-gītā

The Hare Kṛṣṇa Challenge

Back to Godhead magazine (founder)